AEPA Constitution of the United States and Arizona
33
Teacher Certification Exam

By: Sharon Wynne, M.S
Southern Connecticut State University

"And, while there's no reason yet to panic, I think it's only prudent that we make preparations to panic."

XAMonline, INC.
Boston

XAMonline, Inc.
21 Orient Ave.
Melrose, MA 02176
Toll Free 1-800-301-4647
Email: info@xamonline.com
Web www.xamonline.com
Fax: 1-781-662-9268

Library of Congress Cataloging-in-Publication Data

Wynne, Sharon A.
    Constitution of the United States and Arizona 33: Teacher Certification
    / Sharon A. Wynne. -2nd ed. ISBN 978-1-58197-745-5
        1. Constitution of the United States and Arizona 33.   2. Study Guides.
        3. AEPA   4. Teachers' Certification & Licensure.   5. Careers

Disclaimer:
The opinions expressed in this publication are the sole works of XAMonline and were created independently from the National Education Association, Educational Testing Service, or any State Department of Education, National Evaluation Systems or other testing affiliates.

Between the time of publication and printing, state specific standards as well as testing formats and website information may change that is not included in part or in whole within this product. Sample test questions are developed by XAMonline and reflect similar content as on real tests; however, they are not former tests. XAMonline assembles content that aligns with state standards but makes no claims nor guarantees teacher candidates a passing score. Numerical scores are determined by testing companies such as NES or ETS and then are compared with individual state standards. A passing score varies from state to state.

Printed in the United States of America

AEPA: Constitution of the United States and Arizona 33
ISBN: 978-1-58197-745-5

Table of Contents

Great Study and Testing Tips!

What to study in order to prepare for the subject assessments is the focus of this study guide but equally important is *how* you study.

You can increase your chances of truly mastering the information by taking some simple, but effective steps.

Study Tips:

1. Some foods aid the learning process. Foods such as milk, nuts, seeds, rice, and oats help your study efforts by releasing natural memory enhancers called CCKs (*cholecystokinin*) composed of *tryptophan*, *choline*, and *phenylalanine*. All of these chemicals enhance the neurotransmitters associated with memory. Before studying, try a light, protein-rich meal of eggs, turkey, and fish. All of these foods release the memory enhancing chemicals. The better the connections, the more you comprehend.

Likewise, before you take a test, stick to a light snack of energy boosting and relaxing foods. A glass of milk, a piece of fruit, or some peanuts all release various memory-boosting chemicals and help you to relax and focus on the subject at hand.

2. Learn to take great notes. A by-product of our modern culture is that we have grown accustomed to getting our information in short doses (i.e. TV news sound bites or USA Today style newspaper articles.)

Consequently, we've subconsciously trained ourselves to assimilate information better in neat little packages. If your notes are scrawled all over the paper, it fragments the flow of the information. Strive for clarity. Newspapers use a standard format to achieve clarity. Your notes can be much clearer through use of proper formatting. A very effective format is called the *"Cornell Method."*

> Take a sheet of loose-leaf lined notebook paper and draw a line all the way down the paper about 1-2" from the left-hand edge.

> Draw another line across the width of the paper about 1-2" up from the bottom. Repeat this process on the reverse side of the page.

Look at the highly effective result. You have ample room for notes, a left hand margin for special emphasis items or inserting supplementary data from the textbook, a large area at the bottom for a brief summary, and a little rectangular space for just about anything you want.

3. <u>Get the concept then the details</u>. Too often we focus on the details and don't gather an understanding of the concept. However, if you simply memorize only dates, places, or names, you may well miss the whole point of the subject.

A key way to understand things is to put them in your own words. If you are working from a textbook, automatically summarize each paragraph in your mind. If you are outlining text, don't simply copy the author's words.

Rephrase them in your own words. You remember your own thoughts and words much better than someone else's, and subconsciously tend to associate the important details to the core concepts.

4. <u>Ask Why?</u> Pull apart written material paragraph by paragraph and don't forget the captions under the illustrations.

Example: If the heading is "Stream Erosion", flip it around to read "Why do streams erode?" Then answer the questions.

If you train your mind to think in a series of questions and answers, not only will you learn more, but it also helps to lessen the test anxiety because you are used to answering questions.

5. <u>Read for reinforcement and future needs</u>. Even if you only have 10 minutes, put your notes or a book in your hand. Your mind is similar to a computer; you have to input data in order to have it processed. *By reading, you are creating the neural connections for future retrieval.* The more times you read something, the more you reinforce the learning of ideas.

Even if you don't fully understand something on the first pass, *your mind stores much of the material for later recall.*

6. <u>Relax to learn so go into exile</u>. Our bodies respond to an inner clock called biorhythms. Burning the midnight oil works well for some people, but not everyone.

If possible, set aside a particular place to study that is free of distractions. Shut off the television, cell phone, and pager and exile your friends and family during your study period.

If you really are bothered by silence, try background music. Light classical music at a low volume has been shown to aid in concentration over other types. Music that evokes pleasant emotions without lyrics is highly suggested. Try just about anything by Mozart. It relaxes you.

7. <u>Use arrows not highlighters</u>. At best, it's difficult to read a page full of yellow, pink, blue, and green streaks. Try staring at a neon sign for a while and you'll soon see that the horde of colors obscure the message.

A quick note, a brief dash of color, an underline, and an arrow pointing to a particular passage is much clearer than a horde of highlighted words.

8. <u>Budget your study time</u>. Although you shouldn't ignore any of the material, *allocate your available study time in the same ratio that topics may appear on the test.*

Testing Tips:

1. **Get smart, play dumb. Don't read anything into the question.** Don't make an assumption that the test writer is looking for something else than what is asked. Stick to the question as written and don't read extra things into it.

2. **Read the question and all the choices *twice* before answering the question.** You may miss something by not carefully reading, and then re-reading both the question and the answers.

If you really don't have a clue as to the right answer, leave it blank on the first time through. Go on to the other questions, as they may provide a clue as to how to answer the skipped questions.

If later on, you still can't answer the skipped ones . . . *Guess.* The only penalty for guessing is that you *might* get it wrong. Only one thing is certain; if you don't put anything down, you will get it wrong!

3. **Turn the question into a statement.** Look at the way the questions are worded. The syntax of the question usually provides a clue. Does it seem more familiar as a statement rather than as a question? Does it sound strange?

By turning a question into a statement, you may be able to spot if an answer sounds right, and it may also trigger memories of material you have read.

4. **Look for hidden clues.** It's actually very difficult to compose multiple-foil (choice) questions without giving away part of the answer in the options presented.

In most multiple-choice questions you can often readily eliminate one or two of the potential answers. This leaves you with only two real possibilities and automatically your odds go to Fifty-Fifty for very little work.

5. **Trust your instincts.** For every fact that you have read, you subconsciously retain something of that knowledge. On questions that you aren't really certain about, go with your basic instincts. **Your first impression on how to answer a question is usually correct.**

6. **Mark your answers directly on the test booklet.** Don't bother trying to fill in the optical scan sheet on the first pass through the test.

Just be very careful not to miss-mark your answers when you eventually transcribe them to the scan sheet.

7. **Watch the clock!** You have a set amount of time to answer the questions. Don't get bogged down trying to answer a single question at the expense of 10 questions you can more readily answer.

THIS PAGE BLANK

Arizona Constitution Outline

Article I DESIGNATION OF BOUNDARIES

The boundaries of the state of Arizona were defines by the Gadsden Treaty. Article I gives the description in detail in terms of latitude and longitude. The country of Mexico is to the south, New Mexico is on the east, Utah is to the north, and Colorado is to the northeast. The Colorado River forms the border between Arizona with Nevada and California on the west. The state legislatures can change these boundaries at any time with the authorization of the U.S. Congress.

Article II DECLARATION OF RIGHTS

Fundamental principles; recurrence to

1. Individual freedoms and the continuation of government are dependent on the fundamental principles.

Political power; purpose of government

2. The power of the government comes from the people and the purpose of the government is to serve and protect the people.

2.1. Victims' bill of rights

A victim of a crime has the right to be treated with respect, dignity and fairness without intimidation. The victim must be informed when the accused or convicted person is released and has the right to be present at any proceedings. The victim has the right to refuse to be interviewed by the defense and has the right to quick restitution.

Supreme law of the land

3. The U.S. Constitution and federal law take precedence over state law.

Due process of law

4. Due process law must be observed without a person suffering from deprivation of life, liberty and property.

Right of petition and of assembly

5. The people have the right of assembly for peaceful purposes.

Freedom of speech and press

6. People may express themselves freely as long as they don't abuse the right.

Oaths and affirmations

7. When an oath is administered, it must be administered in such as way that it is consistent with the beliefs of the person.

Right to privacy

8. A person's privacy and home must not be invaded without the authority of law.

Irrevocable grants of privileges, franchises or immunities

9. There can be no law written granting privileges or immunity for one person.

Self-incrimination; double jeopardy

10. Individuals cannot be forced to incriminate themselves.

Administration of justice

11. Justice is to be openly administered without delay.

Liberty of conscience; appropriations for religious purposes prohibited; religious freedom

12. Religion and the state are to be separated. No public monies can go for religious purposes. There can be no religious requirements for any office.

Equal privileges and immunities

13. All laws must apply equally to all people and corporations.

Habeas corpus

14. The state cannot suspend the writ of habeas corpus.

Excessive bail; cruel and unusual punishment

15. Cruel and unusual punishment and excessive bail are not allowed.

Corruption of blood; forfeiture of estate

16. A person convicted of a crime cannot be deprived of his inheritance.

Eminent domain; just compensation for private property taken; public use as judicial question

17. If private property is taken for public use just compensation must take place. The amount must be determined by a jury unless the individual agrees to the amount.

Imprisonment for debt

18. Imprisonment for debt only occurs when fraud is evident.

Bribery or illegal rebating; witnesses; self-incrimination no defense

19. If an individual knows of anyone involved in bribery or corruption they are required to give evidence. That person's testimony may not be used against him.

Military power subordinate to civil power

20. The state's civil powers are higher than the military.

Free and equal elections

21. There is to be no interference with free elections by government or the military.

Bailable offenses

22.1. Bail exists for all offenses except capital offenses, felony offenses when the individuals already out on bail, felony offenses where the accused represents a danger to others. The purpose of the bail is to guarantee the appearance of the accused, protect against intimidation of witnesses and to protect the safety of the victim.

Trial by jury; number of jurors specified by law

23. The accused has the right to a trial by jury. There must be twelve jurors on the jury in cases involving death or imprisonment of thirty years and consent among jurors must be unanimous.

Rights of accused in criminal prosecutions

24. The accused has the right to a speedy trial with counsel, and the right to have witnesses for and against him. The accused has the right of appeal if convicted.

Bills of attainder; ex post facto laws; impairment of contract obligations

25. Retroactive laws cannot be enacted nor can a law be enacted to declare a person guilty of a crime (bill of attainder).

Bearing arms

26. Citizens have the rights to bear arms but not to organize private police forces.

Standing army; quartering soldiers

27. Citizens cannot be forced to house soldiers unless it is during wartime and then the quartering must be consistent with the law.

Treason

28. Engaging in war against the state or aiding its enemies is considered treason against the state. It takes two witnesses against the individual for a conviction of treason.

Hereditary emoluments, privileges or powers; perpetuities or entailments

30. No privileges, compensation or powers shall be granted based on hereditary and no laws shall be enacted granting such.

Indictment or information; preliminary examination

31. There can be no indictment for a felony without a preliminary hearing before a magistrate.

Damages for death or personal injuries

32. There can't be an enactment of legislation to limit damages for personal injury.

Constitutional provisions mandatory

33. The constitution's provisions are mandatory unless they are officially amended.

Reservation of rights

34. The people have various rights even if they aren't stated in the Constitution.

Industrial pursuits by state and municipal corporations

35. Public corporations have the right to engage in industrial activities.

Article III DISTRIBUTION OF POWERS

There are three separate branches of government in Arizona: the legislative, the executive and the judicial. Each branch is separate and distinct from the others. Each has its own powers that can't be exercised by any of the others.

Article IV LEGISLATIVE DEPARTMENT

Legislative authority; initiative and referendum

Part 1

1. The Legislature is made up of two bodies: the Senate and the House of Representatives. The people have the right to enact or reject any actions of the legislature through the voting process. There are two ways for legislation to be put forth through the voting process.
2. The initiative is one method the voters have. A new law measure can be proposed through petitions if ten percent of the voters sign and an amendment can be proposed if fifteen percent of the voters sign.
3. A referendum is when the Legislature or five percent of the voters sign petitions, an items is put to the voters to repeal of change a law enacted by the legislature. Enactment of emergency measures requires approval of two thirds of the legislators in both houses and approval of the governor.
4. Initiative petitions, those petitions submitted under the power of the initiative must be filed with the secretary of state at least four months before the election in order to be on the ballot. Referendum petitions, those filed under the power of the referendum, must be filed with the secretary of state at least ninety days after the end of the legislature which passed the measure.
5. Initiative and referendum measures become law by a majority vote in an election with the approval of the governor.
6. The governor cannot veto a referendum or initiative measure passed by a majority of the voters and the legislature cannot vote to repeal or amend any such measures or referendum. The legislature can appropriate or divert funds for the measure by a three fourths vote of each house.
7. The percentage required for the petitions are based on the number of qualified voters that voted for governor in the last election before the initiative or referendum was filed.
8. Incorporated cities, towns and counties can also use the power of initiative and referendum. Fifteen percent of the voters are required to propose measures on the city, town and county and ten percent are required to propose a referendum on the legislature. The cities and towns define the basis for the determination of the percentages.

9. Initiative and referendum petitions must be sent to the secretary of state for state measures and the clerk of the board of supervisors, city clerk or the equivalent for county, city or town measures. The petitioner must state that he is a qualified elector and that the signatures of the petitioners are verified.
10. Any initiative or referendum petition presented to the secretary of state must have the measures appearing on the ballot in the next general election in the form of a "yes" or "no" manner so the voters can approve or disapprove.
11. All measures must be presented as proposed amendments to the constitution guided by the law.
12. If two or more conflicting measures receive approval, the one receiving the largest number of votes will prevail.
13. After the secretary of state canvases the votes for and against each measure, the governor shall announce the resulting number of votes for and against. The measures receiving a majority of the votes are declared as amendments.
14. The legislature can only supersede the referendum or initiative measure with three fourths vote in each house.
15. The legislature has the right to submit measures to the voters.
16. This section of the constitution is self-executing.
17. The legislature is to provide for penalties for the willful violation of these provisions.

Part 2

1. <u>Senate; House of Representatives; members; special session upon petition of members; congressional and legislative boundaries; citizen commissions</u>

   a. The Senate shall have thirty members, one from each legislative district. The House shall have two members from each of the thirty legislative districts.
   b. A special session of the legislature can be called by presenting the governor a petition with signatures of two thirds of the members of each house.
   c. An independent redistricting commission can be established in any year ending in a one to redefine the legislative districts.
   d. Candidates for the independent redistricting commission are nominated by the commission on appellate court appointments.
   e. The commission on appellate court appointments must establish a pool of twenty-five nominees for the independent redistricting commission.
   f. The House and Senate majority and minority leaders can each make one appointment to the independent redistricting commission.
   g. Any vacancies on the independent redistricting commission are to be filled by appointees by the commission on appellate court appointments commission.

h. The chair of the independent redistricting commission is to be selected and cannot belong to either major political party.
i. The five commissioners will select their own vice-chair.
j. A commission member can be removed by the governor with consent of two thirds of the Senate after received written notice.
k. Any vacancies that occur on the independent redistricting commission are to be filled from a pool of three nominees submitted by the commission on appellate court appointees.
l. A quorum consists of three commissioners and the chair or vice-chair.
m. A commissioner is ineligible for public office or registration as a paid lobbyist for three years after his term.
n. The independent redistricting commission will establish legislative and congressional districts in compliance with the U.S. Constitution.
o. Party registration and voting history can't be used to draw the districts but can be used to test for compliance to the rules.
p. The redrawn districts must be available for comment by the pubic and the legislature for at least thirty days before being made final.
q. These provisions are self-executing.
r. Adequate office space and six million dollars are to be made available to the commission. Future appropriations requests are to be submitted in years ending in eight or nine.
s. The independent redistricting commission can make purchases, enter into contracts and hire staff.
t. The independent redistricting commission has standing in any legal actions.
u. Commission members have a right to reimbursement of expenses.
v. Employees of the department of administration shall not try to influence the redistricting of the independent redistricting commission.
w. A commissioner's duties end when his term ends and the commission's duties end when the plan is completed unless they are involved in litigation.

2. A legislative member must be a U.S. citizen, at least twenty-five years old, an Arizona resident for at least three years, and a county resident for at least a year before his election.
3. Each annual session of the legislature shall begin on the second Monday of January. The governor can call a special session.
4. A member of the legislature cannot work for the United States government.
5. A member of the legislature cannot hold any other position with the state of Arizona or city or county except for school trustee or teacher.
6. Members of the legislature cannot be arrested except for treason, felony and breach of the peace. They can not be sued in any civil process while the legislative is in session.
7. A legislative member cannot be held civilly or criminally liable for anything said in the legislature.
8. Each house establishes its own procedure and selects its own leaders.

9. A quorum is required for each house to do business. If a quorum is not present, absent members can be compelled to attend. An adjournment for more than three days is not allowed without the consent of the other house.
10. Records of the proceedings in each house must be kept and a vote can be requested on any question.
11. Each house may establish its own rules for punishment of its members and may expel them with two-thirds vote.
12. A bill must be read three times on three different days before voting takes place. A measure that is passed must be presented to the governor for approval.
13. There can only be one subject per act and it must be stated in the title.
14. When an act is amended, the entire act or section must be published.
15. A majority of each house is required to pass a bill and the passed bill must be signed by the presiding officer.
16. Any legislative member has the right to protest and have the protest entered in the records.
17. Public employees will never receive any extra compensation from the legislature and their services have been rendered.
18. When there are lawsuits against the state, the legislature decides the manner and court in which they may take place.
19. There are no local or special laws regarding divorces, changing county seats, changing rules of evidence, changing laws of succession, regulating the practices of the courts, limitation of civil actions, punishment of crimes, location and building of public thoroughfares, assessment and collection of taxes, regulation of interest rates, the conduction of elections, estates of deceased, granting special privileges, remittance of fines, changing of names, regulation of the functions of justices of the peace, incorporation and amendment of city charters, forgiveness of debt to the state, summoning of juries, or when a general law becomes functional.
20. Only departments of the state, state institutions, public schools, and public debt interest payments can be covered in the general appropriations bill. Any other appropriations have to be presented in separate bills.
21. Members of the legislature serve two year terms. A state senators and representatives cannot serve more than four consecutive terms and must be out of office for one full term before running again for that office.
22. The legislature, or the people by referendum or initiative, have the right to enact laws against juveniles governed by the following: (1) a juvenile over the ages of fifteen accused of a violent crime is prosecuted as an adult; (2) if the juvenile is not a violent or habitual offender the county attorney can recommend other community-based alternatives; (3) all proceedings are matters of public record.
23. Public officers may not accept offers of transportation privileges. They must pay the same rate as the public.

24. The wording of every bill must begin with "Be it enacted by the Legislature of the State of Arizona". The wording of every bill emanating from initiative must begin with "Be it enacted by the People of the State of Arizona."
25. In times of emergency due to enemy attack the legislature can provide for temporary succession of powers for public offices and take actions to insure the continuity of government.

Article V EXECUTIVE DEPARTMENT

Executive department; state officers; terms; election; residence and office at seat of government; duties (Version amended by 1992 Proposition 100)

1. The governor, secretary of state, state treasurer, attorney general and superintendent of public instruction hold office for four years.

2. The person receiving the largest number of votes wins the election. In the case of a tie, the two houses elect one of the people.

3. The officers of the Executive Department must reside at and maintain their offices at the seat of government.

Eligibility to State Offices

2. Executive branch officers must be at least twenty-five years of age and been a U.S. citizen for at least ten years and a citizen of Arizona for at least five years.

Governor, commander-in-chief of the military forces

3. The governor is the commander in chief of the state military unless they are called into service by the United States.

Governor; powers and duties; special sessions of legislature; message and recommendations

4. The governor transacts all of the state's business with the government and the civil and military authorities

Reprieves, commutations and pardons

5. The governor can grant reprieves commutation, and pardons for all offenses except treason and cases of impeachment.

Death, resignation, removal or disability of governor; succession to office; impeachment, absence from state or temporary disability

6. If the governor dies, resigns, is removed from office or is permanently disabled, the secretary of state will assume the office until a special election is held. If the secretary of state can't qualify, then the succession ordering is attorney general, state treasurer or the superintendent of public instruction. In the case of disability, the succession is the same but only until the disability ends.

Presentation of bills to governor; approval; veto; filing with secretary of state; veto of items in appropriation bills; inapplication of veto power to referred bills

7. The governor must sign a bill into law. If the governor doesn't sign, it is returned to the house in which it originated. The governor's objections are entered into the journal. If the bill is passed again in spite of the objections of the governor, it becomes law. This section does not apply to emergency measures. The governor may sign a bill but still object to certain parts of appropriations. This objection must be detailed and the legislature can override the veto. The governor cannot veto a billed referred to the voters.

Vacancies in office

8. The governor can fill any vacancy if there is nothing provided by the law.

Powers and duties of state officers

9. The secretary of state, state treasurer, attorney-general, superintendent of public instruction has powers as prescribed by law.

Canvass of election returns for state officers; certificates of election

10. All election ballots for state officers must be canvassed. The secretary of state must issue certificates of election as provided by law.

Commissions

11. Commission has to issue in the name of the state and must be signed by the governor with the state seal and attested by the secretary of state.

Compensation of elective state officers; commission on salaries for elective state officers

12. Salaries for state officials are as determined by law and may by adjusted in accordance with the law.

Article VI JUDICIAL DEPARTMENTS

Judicial power; courts

1. The judicial consists of a supreme court, intermediate appellate courts, a superior court and such courts inferior to the superior court and justice courts.

Supreme Court; composition; divisions; decisions, transaction of business

2. At least five justices serve on the Supreme Court. The number can be changed by law. They must sit in banc when declaring a law unconstitutional and the decisions must be in writing.

Supreme Court; administrative supervision; chief justice

3. All of the courts in Arizona fall under the administrative supervision of the Supreme Court. The justices elect their own chief justice from among their own for a term of five years. They also select a vice chief justice. Either may resign the position without resigning from the court. The chief justice assigns judges to the lower courts.

Supreme Court; term of office

4. The normal term for a chief justice is six years.

Supreme Court; jurisdiction; writs; rules; habeas corpus

5. The supreme courts has original jurisdiction over writs like habeas corpus, and quo warranto, mandamus, and injunctions; jurisdiction to hear cases between counties concerning disputes of boundaries and claims against one another; appellate jurisdiction from actions originating in courts not of record, unless it is concerned with the validity of a tax impost, assessment, toll, statute or municipal ordinance; the power to grants writs of mandamus, review, prohibition, habeas corpus, certiorari , etc. to fulfill its appellate and revisory functions; the power to make whatever rules it requires in procedural matters; and other jurisdictions provided by law. Writs can be issued to any part of the state.

Supreme Court; qualifications of justices

6. A justice on the Supreme Court must be a resident of Arizona for ten years before taking office and must be of good moral character and qualified to practice law.

<u>Supreme Court; clerk and assistants; administrative director and staff</u>

7. The Supreme Court appoints its own staff like the clerk and administrative director and staff with the amount of compensation determined by law.

<u>Supreme Court; publication of opinions</u>

8. The opinions of the Supreme Court must published and given freely to any person.

<u>Intermediate appellate courts</u>

9. Any intermediate appellate court's jurisdiction, powers, duties and composition are as provided by law.

<u>Superior court; number of judges</u>

10. Each country will have at least one judge of the superior court and more as needed but not more than one judge for each thirty thousand inhabitants.

<u>Superior court; presiding judges; duties</u>

11. Each county shall have a presiding judge of the superior court. If a county has more than two judges, then one is appointed as presiding judge by the Supreme Court. The presiding judge has administrative supervisory capacity over the lower courts.

<u>Superior court; term of office</u>

12. If a county population is less than two hundred fifty thousand persons elect the judge of the superior court to a term of four years. The names of candidates for judge are placed on the regular ballot. Any vacancy that occurs is filled by an appointee of the governor until the next regular election.

<u>Superior court; composition; salaries; judgments and proceedings; process</u>

13. The superior court is a single court with all of its judges with salaries determined by the legislature. One judge's judgments, decrees, orders and proceedings have the same effect as any of the other judges. The process of the court shall extend to all parts of the state.

Superior court; original jurisdiction

14. The superior court has original jurisdiction in the following:

- In cases and proceedings where jurisdiction is not with another court.
- Cases involving the title to real property or the legality of any tax, impost, assessment, toll or municipal ordinance.
- Cases where the value of the property is over one thousand dollars, without interest and costs.
- Criminal cases of felony and misdemeanor not provided for elsewhere.
- Where there is forcible entry and detainer.
- Insolvency proceedings.
- Abatement and prevention of nuisance.
- Probate issues.
- Divorce and annulments.
- Issuance of papers for naturalization.
- Special cases and other jurisdictions as provided by the lay.

Jurisdiction and authority in juvenile proceedings

15. The authority and jurisdiction of the courts regarding juveniles is as provided by the legislature or by the people through initiative or referendum.

Superior court; appellate jurisdiction

16. The superior court has the appellate jurisdiction for the lower courts beneath it.

Superior court; conduct of business; trial juries; jury trial; grand juries

17. Superior courts are always open for the non-jury civil cases and the transaction of business. Parties may waive trial by jury. If not, the jury is to be drawn from the body of the county. A grand jury can only be held by order of the superior court.

Superior court; writs

18. Any judge of the superior court can issue writs of mandamus, quo warranto, review, certiorari, prohibition, and writs of habeas corpus for any person held within the county. These may be issued and served on legal holidays and non-judicial days.

Superior court; service of judge in another county

19. The chief justice of the Supreme Court may direct a judge of the superior court to serve in another county at the request of the presiding judge of the superior court.

Retirement and service of retired justices and judges

20. The basis and pay for the retirement of judges and justices is determined by the legislature. The retirement age is seventy. A retired justice or judge may still serve on any court with reimbursement for his expenses if it is outside his country of residence. He will receive regular compensation for his period of service.

Superior court; speedy decisions

21. A judge of the superior court has sixty days to hand down his decision. If the decision goes over that amount of time, the Supreme Court will provide for speedy disposition.

Superior and other courts; qualifications of judges

22. Judges of the superior court and lower courts must be at least thirty years of age, lived in the state for five years preceding their office, must be or good moral character and admitted to the practice of law in the state.

Superior court; clerk

23. Each county will have a clerk of the superior court who is elected by the voters of the county for a term of four years. The compensation of the clerk is determined by law.

Superior court; court commissioners, masters and referees

24. Superior court judges can appoint court commissioners, masters and referees who will function in accordance with the law and receive such compensation as provided by law.

Style of process; conduct of prosecutions in name of state

25. "The State of Arizona" is the style of process and prosecutions will be conduction in its name and by its authority.

Oath of office

26. A sworn oath to support the United States and Arizona Constitutions must be sworn to by each justice, judge and justice of the peace before they can perform the duties of their office. The oaths of courts inferior to the superior court shall be filed in the office of the county recorder.

Charge to juries; reversal of causes for technical error

27. Judge shall declare the law, not charge juries with matters of fact. No case can be reversed for technical error if it appears that substantial justice has been done.

Justices and judges; dual office holding; political activity; practice of law

28. Judges and justices cannot hold any other public office or employment during their term. They cannot practice law or take part in any political campaign. If a justice or judge files papers to run for public office other than for judge of the superior court, in a county of less than two hundred fifty thousand people, he forfeits his judicial office.

Courts of record

30. The courts of record are the Supreme Court, the court of appeals and the superior court. Others can be established by justice courts and are not courts of record. All other judges from inferior courts are appointed in the manner discussed in section 37 below.

Judges pro tempore

31. The legislature can appoint member of the bar as judges pro tempore of courts below the Supreme Court as provided in section 22. The pro tempore justices do not have to live in the precinct where they serve. They have all of the judicial powers or an elected judge and receive compensation as provided by law.

Justices of the peace and inferior courts; jurisdiction, powers and duties; terms of office; salaries

32. The law states how many justices of the peace are to be elected. The jurisdiction, powers and duties of courts inferior to the superior court and the terms of the judges are as provided by law. The legislature may classify counties and precincts for the purpose of salary determination. The civil jurisdiction can't be greater than ten thousand dollars, without interest and costs. Misdemeanors are the extent of the criminal jurisdiction.

Change by legislature in number of justices or judges; reduction of salary during term of office

33. The legislature cannot change the number of justices and judges that results in removal from office. They also cannot reduce the salary level during his term.

Absence of judicial officer from state

34. If a judicial officer leaves the state for more than sixty days, he forfeits his office unless the governor has extended the leave of absence.

Continuance in office; continued existence of offices; application of prior statute and rules

35. Justices, judges and justices of the peace and officers of the court serve for the term length that they are elected for. Adoption of this article cannot cause any office to be abolished. All persons will serve for the length of the term to which they were appointed. If a vacancy occurs, the appointed will be made subject to section 37 below.

Commission on appellate court appointments and terms, appointments and vacancies on commission

36. A nonpartisan commission on appellate court appointments will consist of the chief justice of the Supreme Court, five attorneys nominated by the board of governors of the Arizona state bar and appointed by the governor and ten nonattorney members appointed by the governor. The governor also appoints members to fill vacancies in a manner that reflects the diversity of the population. They cannot hold any governmental office. The committee reviews applications and sends them to the governor with their recommendations. Attorneys on the commission must have been Arizona residents and practicing before the Supreme Court for at least five years. There can't be more than three attorneys and they can't be members of the same political party. Nonattorneys have to fulfill a five year residency requirement and can't be governmental employees. There can't be more than five of them and they can't be from the same county or political party. Four year terms for both attorneys and nonattorneys are staggered. Only the chief justice can belong to more than one judicial appointment commission. The composition of the commission should reflect the diversity of the population.

Two-thirds of the commission members must be present for an executive session. Voting is in a public hearing. After the public hearings the Supreme Court will provide rules of procedure.

Judicial vacancies and appointments; initial terms; residence; age

37. Within sixty days of a vacancy the commission submits a list of at least three names to the governor as candidates to fill the vacant position. No more than two can be from the same political party. This is the same procedure for a vacancy in the office of judge of the superior court or lower courts. The nominees must be less than sixty-five years of age. The voters vote for retention or rejection of judges of the superior court as provided in section 38. The governor makes the appointment of justices and judges in courts of record when a vacancy occurs. The primary consideration is merit by the diversity of the population is also to be taken into consideration. If the governor doesn't make the appointment in sixty days, the chief justice of the Supreme Court will appoint one of the nominees on the basis of merit. If the commission does not submit a list of nominees within sixty days, the governor can appoint any qualified person to fill the vacancy. The term is to last for two years until sixty days after the election. For intermediate appellate courts or other courts of record, the appointee must be a resident of the country for at least one year and must be less than sixty-five years of age.

Declaration of candidacy; form of judicial ballot, rejection and retention; failure to file declaration

38. Justices or judges of the Supreme Court or intermediate appellate court must file a declaration to retain his office at least sixty days before the end of his term. If not, the term expires and the position becomes vacant. The secretary of state must certify the names to the boards of supervisors so that the name is placed on the ballot in the form of a "yes" or "no" question as to whether the individual should be retained. If the majority of votes are "no", then a vacancy will exist when the term expires. If the majority vote "yes", then the judge or justice serves another term. The secretary of state or the clerk of the board of supervisors will deliver a certificate of retention or rejection to the incumbent based on the counting of the votes.

Retirement of justices and judges; vacancies

39. Justices and judges retire at the age of seventy in accordance with section 35 of this article. The position becomes vacant upon the holder's death, voluntary retirement and as provided in article 38 the expiration of his term. This section is alternative to and cumulative with parts 1 and 2 of article 8 and article 6.1 of this Constitution.

Option for counties with less than two hundred fifty thousand persons

40. Counties with a population of less than two hundred fifty thousand persons may select their judges of the superior courts or of lower courts in the same manner as those counties with populations greater than two hundred fifty thousand persons. If the voters approve, the provisions of sections 12, 28, 30, 35 through 39, 41 and 42 will apply as if such county had a population of two hundred fifty thousand persons or more.

Superior court divisions; commission on trial court appointments; membership; terms

41. Judges of the superior court hold office for a term of four years. There will be a nonpartisan commission on trial court appointment in counties with a population of two hundred fifty thousand persons or more that will consist of the chief justice of the Supreme Court, five attorney members who reside in the district and are members of the bar. They are appointed by the governor subject to confirmation by the senate. There are ten nonattorney members with no more than two from the same district. When there is a vacancy for a nonattorney position, the committee will submit a list to the governor who will appoint two persons from the same district but from different political parties subject to senate confirmation. The composition of the commission should reflect the diversity of the population. Members serve four year staggered terms. Attorney members must have lived in the state and have been admitted to practice by the Supreme Court for at least five years and for one year in the district to which they are appointed. Nonattorney members must have lived in the state for at least five years and the district for at least a year. They cannot be government employees. Members are not eligible to hold a government office or judicial appointment for a one after their term expires. The chief justice is the only person who can serve on more than one judicial appointment commission.

The commission submits to the governor the names of three persons as candidates for the position of judge of the superior court pursuant to section 37 of this article, after holding public hearings and taking testimony. Voting is to be in a public hearing. The Supreme Court will adopt rules of procedure for the commission on trial court appointments. Members of the commission appointed pursuant to section 36 prior to the date of this section serve until their terms expire.

Retention evaluation of justices and judges

42. Justices and judges who file a declaration to be retained are evaluated. The public has the opportunity to participate through public hearings

Article VI.I COMMISSION ON JUDICIAL CONDUCT

Composition; appointment; term; vacancies

1. The commission on judicial conduct consists of eleven periods: two judges from each of the court of appeals, superior court and once justice of the peace and one municipal court judge which is appointed by the supreme court, two member of the state bar appointed by the bar association and three citizens who are not from the legal profession and appointed by the governor subject to senate confirmation. Terms are for six years.

Disqualification of judge

2. A judge is disqualified if there is a pending indictment or a felony charge under Arizona for federal law or a recommendation for his suspension, removal or retirement.

Suspension or removal of judge

3. The supreme court can suspend a judge from office on recommendation of the commission on judicial conduct if he pleads guilty or no contest of is found guilty of a felony under Arizona or federal law or any crime involving moral turpitude. The suspension reverses if the conviction is reversed. He is removed from office if the conviction becomes final.

Retirement of judge

4. The Supreme Court can retire a judge for disability that interferes with this performance of duties. On recommendation of the commission on judicial conduct, they can censure, suspend without pay or remove a judge for willful misconduct in office, willful and persistent failure to perform his duties. If the judge is retired, it is considered to be retired voluntarily. If the judge is removed he is ineligible for judicial office.

Definitions and rules implementing article

5. The term "judge" refers to all justices of the peace, judges in courts inferior to the superior court, judges of the superior court and court of appeals and justices of the Supreme Court. A judge cannot participate in any proceedings involving his own censure, suspension, removal or involuntary retirement.

Article self-executing

6. The provisions of this article are self-executing.

Article VII SUFFRAGE AND ELECTIONS

Method of voting; secrecy

1. People are to vote by use of ballots.

Qualifications of voters; disqualification

2. Voters must be United States citizens, eighteen years of age or over, and have lived in the state for the specified period of time. The right to vote cannot be denied on account of sex. Both males and females have the right to register, vote and hold office. People cannot vote if they are legally declared incapacitated or convicted of treason or felony.

Voting residence of federal employees and certain others

3. Residency cannot be gained or lost due to a person being present or absent while employed in the service of the United States or while a student at any institution or while kept at any institution or other shelter at public expense or while in jail.

Privilege of electors from arrest

4. Except in cased of treason, felony, and breach of the peace, electors shall be privileged from arrest while voting and traveling to and from the voting place.

Military duty on day of election

5. Unless there is a war or public danger, elected are exempt from military duty on the day of an election.

Residence of military personnel stationed within state

6. Military personnel stationed in Arizona are considered residents of the state.

Highest number of votes received as determinative of person elected

7. The candidate receiving the highest number of qualified votes is the winner in an election.

Qualifications for voters at school elections

8. Qualifications for voters for school elections are as provided by law.

Advisory vote

9. Names of candidates for senator are placed on the ballot for the primary elections preceding the general election of the United States senator.

Direct primary election law

10. The legislature enacts the laws providing for direct primary elections for all state, county and city offices and for U.S. senator and representative. Persons with no party preference, independents or with a political party that is not qualified for representation on the ballot may vote in the primary for one of the political parties.

General elections; date

11. The general elections for congress and state, county and precinct officers is to be held on the first Tuesday after the first Monday in November of the first even numbered year after Arizona was admitted to statehood and biennially after that.

Registration and other laws

12. Voters must be registered to vote in accordance with the laws governing elections.

Submission of questions upon bond issues or special assessments

13. Bond issues and special assessments will be voted on by qualified votes in the State.

Fee for placing candidate's name on ballot

14. There is no fee involved for placing a candidate's name on the ballot.

Qualifications for public office

15. Any person elected or appointed to an elective office must be a qualified elector in the political division or municipality where the person was elected.

Campaign contributions and expenditures; publicity

16. All campaign contributions and expenditures must be publicly disclosed by all candidates.

<u>Vacancy in Congress</u>

17. There will be a primary and general election for the nomination and election of United States senator and representative whenever a vacancy occurs.

<u>Term limits on ballot appearances in congressional elections.</u>

18. Term limits are two consecutive terms for U.S. senator and three consecutive terms for U.S. representative.

Article VIII REMOVAL FROM OFFICE

<u>Officers subject to recall; petitioners</u>

1. Every elective public officer in the State of Arizona is subject to public recall by the voters of the district where the officer was elected. Twenty-five percent of the electors that voted for that office are required as petitioners on the recall petition.

<u>Recall petitions; contents; filing; signatures; oath</u>

2. Recall petitions must contain a statement of the reasons for the recall. Each signer must have a signature, date and address of place of residence. The person circulating the petition must sign an oath saying that the signatures are genuine.

<u>Resignation of officer; special election</u>

3. When a vacancy exists due to resignation, the vacancy is filled as provided by law. If more than five days passes after a recall petition is filed and the individual doesn't resign, a special election will be held to determine if the officer should be recalled. The grounds for the recall must be included on the ballot. The individual then remains in office until the results of the election are officially declared.

<u>Special election; candidates; results; qualification of successor</u>

4. The incumbent's name will be placed on the ballot unless he indicates otherwise in writing. The winner of the election is the candidate who receives the highest number of votes. If the incumbent doesn't receive the highest number of votes he is then replaced by the successor. If the successor does not qualify within five days, the office will be filled as provided by law.

<u>Recall petitions; restrictions and conditions</u>

5. There can be no recall petition unless the officer has held office for at least six months, unless he is a member of the legislature in which case it is five days after the beginning of the first session. There can be only one recall petition against the same person during the term unless the petitioners pay the expenses.

<u>Application of general election laws; implementary legislation</u>

6. Recall elections are subject to the general election laws.

<u>Part 2 Power of impeachment in House of Representatives; trial by senate</u>

1. The house of representative has powers of impeachment which requires a majority of all members. The senate has the responsibility for the impeachment trial presided over by the chief justice.

<u>Conviction; grounds for impeachment; judgment; liability to trial</u>

2. A concurrence of two thirds of the senate is required for conviction. The governor and other judicial and state offices, except for justices of courts not of record are liable to impeachment for high crimes, misdemeanors or malfeasance in office. The senate's duties go no further than removal from office. The individual is liable to trial and punishment according to the law.

Article IX PUBLIC DEBT, REVENUE AND TAXATION

<u>Surrender of power of taxation; uniformity of taxes</u>

1. All taxes must be uniform on the same class of property and colleted for public use.

<u>Property subject to taxation; exemptions</u>

1. All federal, state, county and municipal property is exempt from taxation.

2. Non-profit educational, charitable and religious associations or institutions property is exempt from taxation.

3. The public debts and bonds of the state, counties, municipalities or other subdivisions are exempt from taxation.

4. Household goods not used for commercial purposes are exempt from taxation.

5. Business raw materials and inventories if used for resale are exempt from taxation

6. Property used for agricultural use may be exempted from taxation by the legislature but not to more than $50,000.

7. The legislature may make cemeteries tax exempt

11. The property of widows is exempt if the amount of:

    A. $1,500 if the total assessment does not exceed $3,500.

    B. $1,000 if the total assessment does not exceed $4,000.

    C. 500 if the total assessment does not exceed $4,500.

    D. $250 if the total assessment does not exceed $5,000.

    E. No exemption if the total assessment exceeds $5,000.

To qualify for this exemption the income of the widow and the children cannot exceed:

1. $7,000 if none of the children under eighteen resided in the widow's residence.

2. $10,000 if the one or more of the widow's children residing in her residence is eighteen and disabled physically or mentally.

    The widow must have been living with her spouse at the time of this death before January 1, 1969.

12. The total exemption will not exceed $1,500. The provisions of this section shall be self-executing.

13. Property that is not exempt is subject to taxation as provided by law.

Exemption from tax; property of persons who are disabled

2.2 A. The property an individual over the age of seventeen that is totally and permanently disabled in the amount of:

1. $1,500 if the total assessment does not exceed $3,500.

2. $1,000 if the total assessment does not exceed $4,000.

3. $500 if the total assessment does not exceed $4,500.

4. $250 if the total assessment does not exceed $5,000.

5. If the total assessment exceeds $5,000, there is no exemption.

B. The exemption only applies when all income in the person's residence doesn't exceed:

1. $7,000 in none of the person's under eighteen years of ages children reside in the residence.

2. $10,000 if one or more of the children under eighteen and residing in the residence is totally and permanently disabled.

C. The total exemption cannot exceed $1,500. This section is self-executing.

Exemption from tax; increase in amount of exemptions, assessments and income

2.3. The legislature can change the exemptions, the amounts of the assessments or the among of income allowed in sections 2, 2.3 and 2.2 of this article

Annual tax; purposes; amount; tax laws; payment of taxes into state treasury

3. The legislature shall provide for the collection of taxes sufficient to cover the expenses of government and to cover the public debt and interest. Tax revenues are paid to the state treasury.

Fiscal year; annual statement of receipts and expenditures; deficit

4. The fiscal year begins on July 1. The state must publish the statement of receipts and expenditures. In case of a deficit, the legislature may levy taxes to pay the deficiency.

Power of state to contract debts; purposes; limit; restrictions

5. The state may incur debts to supply the deficit in revenues but never more than $350,000. The state may raise money and incur debt to repel invasion, suppress insurrection and to defend the state in time of war.

Local assessments and taxes

6. Incorporated cities, towns, and villages can levy special assessments or special taxation of property to make local improvement.

Gift or loan of credit; subsidies; stock ownership; joint ownership

7. No governmental unit may use public funds for a loan or gift or become an owner or joint owner in any company or corporation except as to such ownership as may accrue to the state as authorized by law.

Local debt limits; assent of taxpayers

8. No county, city, town, school district, or other municipal corporation will acquire debt of more than six percent of the taxable property without consent of the majority of property owners. No district can incur an amount of debt exceeding fifteen percent of the taxable property and even with assent the amount of the debt cannot exceed twenty percent for use for public projects. The provisions of section 18, subsections (3), (4), (5) and (6) of this article do not apply to this section.

Unified school district debt limit

8.1. The debts of a unified school district cannot exceed thirty percent of the taxable property of the district. The provisions of section 18, subsections (3), (4), (5) and (6) of this article do not apply to this section.

Statement of tax and objects

9. Every law imposed for taxes must state the purpose of the tax and what is will be applied to.

Aid of church, private or sectarian school, or public service corporation

10. No public money may aid any church or private or sectarian school or any public service corporation.

Taxing procedure; license tax on registered vehicles

11. After December 3, 1973, a license tax on vehicles will replace the ad valorem property taxes on vehicles. The collection is a provided by law. Mobile homes will have an ad valorem property tax levied as provided by law.

Authority to provide for levy and collection of license and other taxes

12. The law-making power may levy and collect taxes.

Inventory, materials and products of manufacturers; production livestock and animals; tax exemption

13. No tax shall be levied on:

    1. Raw materials, inputs, unfinished parts and inventory.

    2. Livestock, poultry, aquatic animals and honeybees owned by a person engaged in agriculture.

Use and distribution of vehicle, user, and gasoline and diesel tax receipts

14. Moneys derived from fees, excises, or license taxes relating to registration, operation or use of vehicles or to fuels used for vehicles can only be used for highway and streets including the cost of administration. This section does not apply to moneys derived from the automobile license tax imposed under section 11 of article IX of the Constitution of Arizona. All moneys collected in accordance with this section will be distributed as provided by law.

License tax on aircraft

15. Beginning January 1, 1965 a license tax on aircraft will take the place of the ad valorem property tax and will apply to:

    1. Aircraft owned by airlines carrying persons or property in interstate, intrastate or international transportation.

    2. Aircraft owned by a dealer for the purpose of sale.

    3. Noncommercial private aircraft owned by a nonresident that is used ninety days or less per year.

    4. Aircraft owned and operated by the state of subdivision of or by the civil air patrol.

<u>Exemption of watercraft from ad valorem property taxes</u>

16.   All watercraft except those owned and operated for commercial purposes, are exempt from ad valorem property tax but are subject to a license tax.

<u>Economic estimates commission; appropriation limitation; powers and duties of commission</u>

17.   There will not be more than three people on the economic estimates commission that will public the estimated total personal income for the following fiscal year.

(2)   For purposes of this section, state revenues are:

a. All monies, revenues, fees, fines, penalties, funds, tuitions, property and receipts received by the account of the state or any of its agencies, departments, offices, boards, commissions, authorities, councils and institutions. This doesn't include amounts from bonds, payments of dividends or interest, amounts or property received by the state in its capacity of trustee, custodian or agent, deposits for unemployment compensation, funds for distribution to the counties, cities and towns without specific restrictions other than in section 14 of this article.

3.   The legislature cannot appropriate more than seven percent of total personal income as determined by the economic estimates commission unless there is a two-thirds vote of each house.

4.   The legislature can adjust the appropriation percentage consistent with the following:

a.   The appropriation limitation will be decreased is the federal government assumes all or any part of the cost of providing the function

b.   The appropriation limitation will be increased if the state has to assume a function that the federal government previously provided.

c.   A political subdivision will lower the appropriation percentage if the state assumes the providing of a function and it will increase its appropriation limitation.

d.   The state will lower is appropriation percentage if a political subdivision assumes the cost of providing a function.

Adjustments become effective for the first fiscal year after the assumption of the cost.

Residential ad valorem tax limits; limit on increase in values; definitions

18. The maximum amount of ad valorem tax that can be collected can't exceed one per cent of the property's cash value. This does not apply to taxes and assessments to pay bonds, or for property improvement assessment districts, improvement districts and other special purpose districts, or an election that exceeded a budget, expenditure or tax limitation. The legislature provides a method for determining the value of new property. This limitation on increases does not apply to: mining property, oil producing property, real property improvements by utilities, commercial aircraft, timber, pipelines, and personal property.

    A resident who is sixty-five years old or more may apply for a property valuation protection option on the primary residence. He must apply before September 1 and have lived in the residence for at least two years. His total income cannot exceed four hundred percent of the supplemental security income benefit rate. If the property is owned by two or more people, one must be at least sixty-five years of age and their combined income cannot exceed five hundred percent of the supplemental security income benefit rate. The owner's qualifications are reviewed every three years. If the property is approved the value remains fixed at the full cash value of the year that the primary residence protection was granted as long as the owner is eligible. The owner must reapply every three years. It the title is changed to someone who does not qualify for the property valuation protection option, it terminates and the property reverts to its full cash value.

    For purposes of this section owner is the owner of record including a person who is the major beneficial interest of a living trust. Primary residence refers to owner occupied property like a single family residence, condominium, townhouse or mobile home.

Limitation on ad valorem tax levied; exceptions

19. There can't be more than a two percent yearly increase in the ad valorem tax by any country, city, town or community college district.

Expenditure limitation; adjustments; reporting

20. A two-thirds vote of the governing board is required to expenditures or revenues. Approval for excess expenditures requires a majority of voter's approval at a special election. The legislature provides for expenditure limitations as is necessary.

Expenditure limitations for school districts and community college districts

21. The economics estimates commission determines and publishes the expenditure limitation for each community college district and all school districts. Expenditures in excess of this amount may be authorized by two-thirds vote in each house of the legislature.

Vote required to increase state revenues; application; exceptions

22. An increase in state revenues requires a two-third vote of each house of the legislature. If the act is vetoed by the governor, then a three-fourths vote in each house is required to enact the measure. This applies to any new tax, an increase in tax rates, a reduction or elimination of a tax deduction, exemption, exclusion, credit, an increased in a fee or assessment, the imposition or elimination of a new state fee, a change in allocation of taxes.

Expenditures required by initiative or referendum; funding source

23. Any initiative or referendum measure that proposes an expenditure must also provide for an increased source of revenue to cover the expenditure. The funds cannot come from the state general fund or cause a reduction in general fund revenues.

Article 10 STATE AND SCHOOL LANDS

Acceptance and holding of lands by state in trust

1. All lands acquired by the state shall be held in trust.

Unauthorized disposition of land or proceeds as breach of trust

2. If disposition of the lands is contrary to the provisions of the Enabling Act, then there is a breach of trust.

Mortgage or other encumbrance; sale or lease at public auction

3. The lands can only be sold a public auction to the highest bidder with the auction held at the county seat where the land is. Notice of the auction must be published once a week for ten weeks. State lands may be leased for up to ten years without advertisement if used to agricultural, grazing, commercial and homesite purposes. State lands may be leased for twenty years for mineral purposes oil, gas and hydrocarbon purposes.

Sale or other disposal; appraisal; minimum price; credit; passing of title

4. All lands must be sold at their true appraised value and no title transfers until the consideration has been paid.

Minimum price; relinquishment of lands to United States

5. No lands can be sold for less than three dollars per acre and if the land is irrigated, then it can be sold at less than twenty-five dollars per acre.

Lands reserved by United States for development of water power

6. Lands that have been reserved by the United States for development of water power must be designated by the secretary of the interior within five years after the proclamation. After five years, the state may dispose of the lands.

Establishment of permanent funds; segregation, investment and distribution of monies

7. If there is a grant, the state treasurer must deposit the funds in a permanent fund corresponding to the grant under which the particular land was conveyed. No monies may be moved from one permanent fund to another and all monies must be invested in safe interest bearing securities with a trustee appointed by the board of investment. There can't be more than sixty percent invested in stocks and the state cannot invest more than five percent in any one stock. The investment board decides the deposits to and withdraws from the stocks.

Conformity of contracts with enabling act

8. Any action not in accordance with the Enabling Act is null and void.

Sale or lease; conditions; limitations; lease prior to adoption of constitution

9. Lands granted to the state prior to the adoption of the constitution have to be appraised and well as the improvements on school and university lands.

Laws for sale or lease of state lands; protection of residents and lessees

10. Residents and lessees of state land will be paid by the succeeding lessees for the value of any improvements.

Maximum acreage allowed single purchaser

11. No individual, corporation or association shall be allowed to purchase more than one hundred sixty (160) acres of agricultural land or more than six hundred forty (640) acres of grazing land.

Article XI EDUCATION

1. Public school system; education of pupils who are hearing and vision impaired

1. The government will provide for a public school system which will include kindergarten, common schools, high schools, normal schools, industrial schools, and universities, in addition to schools for the hearing and vision impaired.

Conduct and supervision of school system

2. The school system will be run by a state board of education, a state superintendent of public instruction, county school superintendents, and governing boards for the state institutions.

State board of education; composition; powers and duties; compensation

3. The state board of education shall be composed of the superintendent of public instruction, the president of a state university or a state college, four lay members, a president or chancellor of a community college district, a person who is an owner or administrator of a charter school, a superintendent of a high school district, a classroom teacher and a county school superintendent.

State superintendent of public instruction; board membership; powers and duties

4. The state superintendent of public instruction , secretary of the state board of education and a member of any other board having control of public instruction in any state institution.

Regents of university and other governing boards; appointments by governor; membership of governor on board of regents

5. The governor, with consent of the senate, will appoint the regents of the university and the governing boards of other state institutions and the governor will be an ex-officio member of the board of regents of the university.

Admission of students of both sexes to state educational institutions; tuition; common school system

6. All state educational institutions are open to students of both sexes. A free school will be established in every district for at least six months.

Sectarian instruction; religious or political test or qualification

7. There is to be no religious or political test or qualification for any state school.

8. The rental from school land will be used only for common and high school education.

County school fund; size of fund; free schools

9. The legislature shall enact laws that provide for funding the county school fund

Source of revenue for maintenance of state educational institutions

10. The legislature will make appropriations for taxes to provide for the proper maintenance of all state educational institutions.

Article XII COUNTIES

Counties as bodies politic and corporate

1. Every county is a body politic and corporate.

Counties of territory as counties of state

2. Counties are counties of the state until changed by law.

County officers; election; term of office

3. Each county will elect a sheriff, a county attorney, a recorder, a treasurer, an assessor, a superintendent of schools and at least three supervisors who will serve four year terms. The supervisors will be nominated from districts. The terms begin on January 1 following the election.

County officers; duties, powers, and qualifications; salaries

4. The duties of the officers of the county are as prescribed by law. The board of supervisors will determine salaries for all county and precinct officers.

Charter committee; charter preparation; approval

5. A county with a population of more than five hundred thousand people may have a charter committee elected by the voters. The charter committee will have fifteen persons with the same number from each district. Within one hundred eighty days of the election, the charter committee will submit a charter for the county which must be published in the official newspaper once a week for three weeks. The electors vote on the charter as to whether they accept or reject it. When it is ratified it goes to the governor, who has thirty days to approve it. When approved, the charter becomes the organic law of the county.

Amendment of charter

6. Amendments to the charter must be approved by the voters and the governor in accordance with section 5 of this article.

County charter provisions

7. Charter counties are political subdivisions of the state. The county is governed by the terms of its charter. The county may collect taxes on a countywide basis and on a specially designated area basis. New taxes must be authorized by the voters. If provided for in the charter, the county may also adopt a fee schedule for its services.

Government and other powers

8. A. The county charter provides for an elective governing body, the method of compensation, its powers, duties, responsibilities and its authority to delegate powers, the method of election and removal of members, the terms of office and the method for filling vacancies. The charter must be reviewed at least once every ten years.

Self-executing provision

9. The provisions of sections 5 through 8 of this article are self-executing, and no further legislation is required to make them effective.

Article XIII MUNICIPAL CORPORATIONS

Incorporation and organization; classification

1. Municipal corporations are created by the general laws of the legislature that provide for the incorporation of cities and towns.

Charter; preparation and proposal by board of freeholders; ratification and approval; amendment

2. A city or town with more than three thousand five hundred people may frame its own charter for its own government. They elect fourteen qualified electors to a board of freeholders who prepare a charter for the city. The proposed charter must be published for three weeks in a newspaper and then submitted to the voters for ratification. Then the charter is submitted to the governor. If approved, the charter becomes the law of the city.

3. The legislative authority of a city can call for the election of a board of freeholders at any time there is a petition presented signed by twenty five percent of the voters.

Franchises; approval of electors; term

4. A franchise cannot be granted, extended or renewed without the approval of a majority of the voters. Franchises cannot be granted, extended or renewed for a period over twenty-five years.

Right of municipal corporation to engage in business or enterprise

5. Municipal corporations have the right to engage in business.

Franchises; restrictions

6. Municipal corporations cannot divest the state or any of their subdivisions of their control and regulation of streets, alleys or other public grounds. No exclusive franchise can ever be granted.

Irrigation and other districts as political subdivisions

6. Irrigation, power, electrical, agricultural improvement, drainage, and flood control districts, and tax levying public improvement districts, are political subdivisions of the state.

Article XIV CORPORATION OTHER THAN MUNICIPAL

"Corporation" defined; right to sue and suability

1. The term corporation includes all associations and joint stock companies. Corporations have the right to sue and be sued.

Formation under general laws; change of laws; regulation

2. Corporations must be formed under general laws.

Existing charters

3. Charters existing at the time of approval of this Constitution have no validity.

Restriction to business authorized by charter or law

4. Corporations can only engage in the business authorized by its charter.

Foreign corporations; transaction of business

5. Foreign corporations cannot transact business on more favorable terms than other corporations.

Stocks; bonds

6. Stock can only be issued to bona fide subscribers. Bonds can only be issued for money or property received or for labor done.

Lease or alienation of franchise

7. The corporation cannot lease or alienate any franchise to relive the franchise of its liabilities.

Filing of articles of incorporation; place of business; agent for service of process; venue

8. The articles of incorporation must be filed with the corporation commission and there must be one or more known places of business and an authorized agent in the state upon whom process may be served. A foreign corporation may be sued in the county where an agent is found on in the county where the cause of action may arise.

Eminent domain; taking corporate property and franchises for public use

9. The state has the right of eminent domain over incorporated companies.

Elections for directors or managers

10. Shareholders have the right to vote in elections for directors or managers.

Liability of stockholders

11. The shareholders of banking and insurance corporations are held individually responsible for all contracts, debts and engagements of the corporation to their extent of the amount of their stock holdings.

Officers of banking institutions; individual responsibility

12. A president, director, manager, cashier or other officer of a bank can be held individually responsible for accepting deposits one they have knowledge that the banking institution is insolvent of in failing circumstances.

Want of legal organization as a defense

13. The want of legal organization cannot be used as a defense to any action brought against the corporation.

Legislative power to impose conditions

14. The legislature may impose other conditions upon corporations.

Monopolies and trusts

15. Monopolies and trusts are not allowed in Arizona.

Records, books, and files; visitorial and inquisitorial powers of state

16. The state has the right to review the books, records and files of all public services corporations, state banks, building and loan associations, trust, insurance, and guaranty companies.

Fees; reports; licensing of foreign corporations

17. All corporations must pay an annual fee to the state to register their corporation

Contributions to influence elections or official action

18. Corporations cannot make contributions to elections.

Penalties for violation of article

19. Suitable penalties shall be prescribed by law for the violation of any of the provisions of this article.

Article XV THE CORPORATION COMMISSION

Term limits on corporation commission; composition; election; office vacancies; qualifications

1. A corporation commission member cannot serve more than two consecutive terms. The corporation commission consists of five persons elected at a general election to terms of four years. The governor will appoint an individual to fill a vacancy.

"Public service corporations" defined

2. Public service corporations are corporations that are not municipal and that furnish gas, oil, electricity, sewers, telephone and common carriers.

Power of commission as to classifications, rates and charges, rules, contracts, and accounts; local regulation

3. The corporation commission determines the classifications and rates and charges applying to the public service corporations operating in Arizona. They determine the rules that govern these corporations.

Power to inspect and investigate

4. The corporation commission has to power to inspect and investigate the property, books, papers, business, methods and affairs of corporations that offer stock for sale to the public.

Power to issue certificates of incorporation and licenses

5. Public service corporations must have a certificate of incorporation from the corporation commission to do business in Arizona.

Enlargement of powers by legislature; rules and regulations

6. The corporation commission's powers are as provided by law.

Connecting and intersecting lines of transportation and communications corporations

7. Authorized public service corporations have the right to construct and operate lines connecting points within the state and connect at the state borders with like lines.

Transportation by connecting carriers

8. Public service corporations engaging in transportation will transport without delay or discrimination to other public service corporations.

Transmission of messages by connecting carriers

9. Public service corporations engaged in transmitting messages for profit will receive and transmit messages without delay or discrimination with other public service corporations as proscribed by law or the corporation commission.

Railways as public highways; other corporations as common carriers

10. Railroads are public highways and common carriers subject to control by law. Electric, transmission, telegraph, telephone or pipeline corporations for profit are common carriers and subject to control by law.

Movable property as personal property; liability of property to attachment, execution and sale

11. The public service corporations rolling stock and movable property are considers its personal property and subject to attachment, execution, and sale.

Charges for service; discrimination; free or reduced rate transportation

12. Charges by public service corporations must be just and reasonable with no discrimination in charges, service or facilities

Reports to commission

13. Public service corporations must make reports to the corporation commission and provide the information required by law.

Value of property of public service corporations

14. The corporation commission will determine the fair value of the property of every public service corporation with the assistance of the public service commission as provided by law.

Acceptance of constitutional provisions by existing corporations

15. Public service corporations in existence at the time of the states admission to the union have the benefit of any future legislation upon complete acceptance of the provisions of this Constitution.

Forfeitures for violations

16. Violation of corporation commission rules, regulations, orders or decisions result in a fine between $100 and $5000 for each violation.

Appeal to courts

17. The public service corporation has the right of appeal to the courts for the rules, regulations, orders or decrees of the corporation commission.

<u>Power to impose fines</u>

19. The corporation commission shall have the power and authority to enforce its rules, regulations, and orders by the imposition of such fines as it may deem just, within the limitations prescribed in section 16 of this article.

Article XVI MILITIA

<u>Composition of militia</u>

1. The militia consists of all capable citizens between the ages of eighteen and forty-five years.

<u>Composition and designation of organized militia</u>

2. The militia is known as "The National Guard of Arizona".

<u>Conformity to federal regulations</u>

3. The militia's organization, equipment and discipline must conform to the regulations of the United States military.

Article XVII WATER RIGHTS

<u>Riparian water rights</u>

1. Water rights in the state are not controlled by the common law doctrine of riparian water rights.

<u>Recognition of existing rights</u>

2. The rights existing when Arizona became a state to use the waters in a beneficial manner are recognized and confirmed.

Article XVIII LABOR

<u>Eight-hour day</u>

1. A lawful workday cannot exceed eight hours.

<u>Child labor</u>

2. Children under fourteen years cannot be gainfully employed during the hours of the school day in the district. A child under sixteen years cannot be employed in mines or any occupation that can cause injury to health or morals and cannot work for more than eight hours a day.

Contractual immunity of employer from liability for negligence

3. It is unlawful for any employer to require its employees to sign anything relieving them of liability or responsibility for personal injuries as a result of employment. Any such contract or agreement is null and void.

Fellow servant doctrine

4. The common law doctrine of fellow servant is forever abrogated.

Contributory negligence and assumption of risk

5. The defense of contributory negligence is to be determined by a jury.

Recovery of damages for injuries

6. The injured party has the right to recover damages for injuries and the amount is not subject to any statutory limitation.

Employer's liability law

7. Under the employer's liability law, the employer is liable for the death or injury of an employee incurred while working in the service of the employer where there is no negligence on the part of the employee.

Workmen's compensation law

8. The workmen's compensation law provides compensation to the workman or his dependents if he is injured or killed while working.

Blacklists

9. Blacklists of workers are prohibited.

Employment of aliens

10. If a person is not a United States citizen or ward of such they cannot be employed with any state, county or municipal employment except for prison work or teachers in schools.

ARTICLE XIX MINES

(Version amended by 1992 Proposition 101)

The legislature enacts laws that provide for the health and safety of workers. There is an office of mine inspector who is elected at general election for a four year term.

Article XIX ORDINANCE

(Version amended by 1992 Proposition 107)

The legislature enacts laws regulating the operation and equipment of mines and that provide for the health and safety of workers. The mine inspector will be elected at general elections for a term of two years and cannot serve more than four consecutive terms

Toleration of religious sentiment

First.   Arizona guarantees toleration of all religions to every inhabitant of the state.

Polygamy

Second.   Polygamy or plural marriages are forever prohibited within the state.

Introduction of intoxicating liquors into Indian country

Third.   The reselling of liquor on Indian lands is prohibited until July 1, 1957.

Public lands; Indian lands

Fourth.   The state has no claims on Indian tribal lands which are under the control of the Indian tribes and the United State Congress.

Taxation

Fifth.   Land owned by people residing out-of-state cannot be taxed at higher rates. The state cannot tax land or property on Indian reservations.

Territorial debts and liabilities

Sixth.   The state of Arizona assumed all of the debts and liabilities of territory of Arizona and counties that existed prior to June 20, 1910.

Public school system; suffrage

Seventh. Public school education is open to all children of the state, free of sectarian control and conducted in English. There can never be a law restricting the right to vote on the basis of race, color, or previous condition of servitude.

English language

Eighth. State officers and members of the state legislature must be able to read, write, speak and understand English without the aid of an interpreter.

Location of state capital

Ninth. Phoenix is the capital of Arizona unless it is changed by the voters.

Lands granted to state

Twelfth. The state of Arizona and its people consent to the enabling act of June 20, 1910.

Ordinance as part of constitution; amendment

Thirteenth. This ordinance is part of the Constitution of Arizona and can't be changed without the consent of Congress.

Article XXI MODE OF AMENDING

Introduction in legislature; initiative petition; election

1. Proposed amendments to the constitution can come from either house of the legislature of by initiative petition signed by fifteen percent of the total number of votes for governor in the last election. The proposed amendment is presented to the secretary of state to be included on the ballot at the next general election. The proposed amendment has to be published in the newspaper for a period of ninety days preceding the election. If the amendment is ratified, it becomes a part of the constitution.

Convention

2. There can be no convention called by the Legislature to change this Constitution unless it is approved by the people on a Referendum vote.

Article XXII SCHEDULE AND MISCELLANEOUS

Existing rights, actions, suits, proceedings, contracts, claims, or demands; process

1. What existed under the Territory of Arizona continues under the State of Arizona.

Territorial laws

2. The laws of the Territory of Arizona will continue under the State of Arizona until their expiration.

Debts, fines, penalties, and forfeitures

3. All debts, fines, penalties and forfeitures with the Territory of Arizona accrue to the State of Arizona.

Recognizances; bonds; estate; judgments; choses in action

4. All recognizances and bonds pass from the Territory of Arizona to the State of Arizona.

Criminal prosecutions and penal actions; offenses; penalties; actions and suits

5. All criminal prosecutions and penal actions arising with the Territory of Arizona pass to the State of Arizona.

Territorial, district, county, and precinct officers

6. All Territorial, district, county and precinct officer in office at the time of Arizona's admission to the Union continue in their office until their successors have qualified.

Causes pending in district courts of territory; records, papers, and property

7. Causes pending the district court of the Territory become the jurisdiction of the superior court.

Probate records and proceedings

8. Proceedings of the probate court pass to the jurisdiction of the superior court when this Constitution becomes effective.

Causes pending in supreme court of territory; records, papers, and property

9. Cases pending before the Supreme Court of the Territory pass to the Supreme Court of the State and those that would have been before the United States Courts if they had existed pass into the jurisdiction of the United States courts as provided for in the Enabling Act.

Seals of supreme court, superior courts, municipalities, and county officers

10. The seals will have the word "Territory" replaced by the word State".

Effective date of constitution

11. The provisions of this Constitution become effective the day on which the President of the United State declares the State of Arizona admitted into the Union.

Election of representative in congress

12. One Representative to the Congress will be elected at the same election at which officers shall be elected under the Enabling Act.

Continuation in office until qualification of successor

13. The terms of every office extend until the successor is elected and qualified.

Initiative

14. The people can enact by Initiative any law that the Legislature can enact.

Public institutions

15. The state will support correctional, penal, and institutions for the mentally and physically disabled and other such institutions as required in the manner prescribed by law.

Confinement of minor offenders

16. Minors under eighteen cannot be confined with adults.

Compensation of public officers

17. All State and county officers and justices of the peace and constables will be paid fixed salaries.

Nomination of incumbent public officers to other offices

18. Incumbents of a salaried elective office cannot run for election to any salaried local, state or federal office without first resigning their position unless it is the final year of their term.

Lobbying

19. Lobbying is not allowed on the floor of either house of the legislature by provision of law.

Design of state seal

20. The state seal has a storage reservoir and dam with irrigated fields and orchards with cattle grazing with a background of mountains with the sun rising over the peaks. There is a quartz mill with a miner holding a pick and shovel. There is the motto "Ditat Deus. There is a circular band with the saying "Great Seal of the State of Arizona" with the year of admission into the Union.

Enactment of laws to carry constitution into effect

21. The Legislature enacts all necessary laws to carry into effect the provisions of this Constitution.

Judgments of death

22. The death sentence shall be carried out by administration of a lethal injection or by lethal gas.

Article XXV RIGHT TO WORK

Right to work or employment without membership in labor organization

A person cannot be denied the right to work because he doesn't belong to a labor union.

Powers of real estate broker or salesman

Anyone with a valid real estate broker or salesman license can draft and complete purchase agreements, earnest money receipts, deeds, mortgages, leases, assignments, releases, contracts for sale of realty and bills of sale.

Regulation of ambulances; powers of legislature

1. The legislature provides for the regulation of ambulances and ambulance services.

English as the official language; applicability

1. English is the official language of the state of Arizona and is the language of the ballot, public schools and all government functions and actions. This article applies to the legislative, executive and judicial branches of government and all political subdivisions, all statutes, ordinances, rules, orders, programs and policies and all government officials and employees in the performance of government business.

Requiring this state to preserve, protect and enhance English

2. Reasonable steps must be taken to preserve, protect and enhance the role of English as the official language of Arizona.

Prohibiting this state from using or requiring the use of languages other than English; exceptions

3. A language other than English can be used in the following situations: to help students who aren't proficient in English, to comply with other federal laws, to teach a student a foreign language, to protect public health and safety and to protect the rights of criminal defendants or victims or crime

Enforcement; standing

4. A person has the right to bring suit to enforce this article.

Public Retirement Systems

1. Public retirement systems are funded with contributions and investment earnings. The assets of the public retirement systems are separate and independent funds. The members of a public retirement system have a contractual relationship that cannot be diminished.

Article XXVI RIGHT OF LICENSED REAL ESTATE BROKERS AND SALESMEN TO PREPARE INSTRUMENTS INCIDENT TO PROPERTY TRANSACTIONS

Powers of real estate broker or salesman

1. A real estate broker or salesman can draft or complete, without charge, any and all instruments including preliminary purchase agreements and earnest money receipts, deeds, mortgages, leases, assignments, releases, contracts for sale of realty, and bills of sale.

Article XXVII REGULATION OF PUBLIC HEALTH, SAFETY AND WELFARE

Regulation of ambulances; powers of legislature

1. The legislature provides for the regulation of ambulances and ambulance services in terms of services provided, routes served, response times and charges.

Article XXVIII English as the Official Language

English as the official language; applicability

1. English is the official language of the state of Arizona and is the language of the ballot, public schools and all government functions and actions. This article applies to the legislative, executive and judicial branches of government and all political subdivisions, all statutes, ordinances, rules, orders, programs and policies and all government officials and employees in the performance of government business

Requiring this state to preserve, protect and enhance English

2. 2. Reasonable steps must be taken to preserve, protect and enhance the role of English as the official language of Arizona.

Prohibiting this state from using or requiring the use of languages other than English; exceptions

3. A language other than English can be used in the following situations: to help students who aren't proficient in English, to comply with other federal laws, to teach a student a foreign language, to protect public health and safety and to protect the rights of criminal defendants or victims or crime

Enforcement; standing

4. A person has the right to bring suit to enforce this article.

Article XXIX PUBLIC RETIREMENT SYSTEMS

Public retirement systems

1. Public retirement systems are funded with contributions and investment earnings. The assets of the public retirement systems are separate and independent funds. The members of a public retirement system have a contractual relationship that cannot be diminished.

Constitution

Preamble

We, the people of the State of Arizona, grateful to Almighty God for our liberties, do ordain this Constitution.

Article I

DESIGNATION OF BOUNDARIES

Section 1. The boundaries of the State of Arizona shall be as follows, namely: Beginning at a point on the Colorado River twenty English miles below the junction of the Gila and Colorado Rivers, as fixed by the Gadsden Treaty between the United States and Mexico, being in latitude thirty-two degrees, twenty-nine minutes, forty-four and forty-five one- hundredths seconds north and longitude one hundred fourteen degrees, forty-eight minutes, forty-four and fifty-three one -hundredths seconds west of Greenwich; thence along and with the international boundary line between the United States and Mexico in a southeastern direction to Monument Number 127 on said boundary line in latitude thirty-one degrees, twenty minutes north; thence east along and with said parallel of latitude, continuing on said boundary line to an intersection with the meridian of longitude one hundred nine degrees, two minutes, fifty-nine and twenty-five one-hundredths seconds west, being identical with the southwestern corner of New Mexico; thence north along and with said meridian of longitude and the west boundary of New Mexico to an intersection with the parallel of latitude thirty-seven degrees north, being the common corner of Colorado, Utah, Arizona, and New Mexico; thence west along and with said parallel of latitude and the south boundary of Utah to an intersection with the meridian of longitude one hundred fourteen degrees, two minutes, fifty-nine and twenty-five one-hundredths seconds west, being on the east boundary line of the State of Nevada; thence south along and with said meridian of longitude and the east boundary of said State of Nevada, to the center of the Colorado River; thence down the mid-channel of said Colorado River in a southern direction along and with the east boundaries of Nevada, California, and the Mexican Territory of Lower California, successively, to the place of beginning.

2. Alteration of state boundaries

Section 2. The legislature, in cooperation with the properly constituted authority of any adjoining state, is empowered to change, alter, and redefine the state boundaries, such change, alteration and redefinition to become effective only upon approval of the Congress of the United States.

Article II

DECLARATION OF RIGHTS

1. Fundamental principles; recurrence to

Section 1. A frequent recurrence to fundamental principles is essential to the security of individual rights and the perpetuity of free government.

2. Political power; purpose of government

Section 2. All political power is inherent in the people, and governments derive their just powers from the consent of the governed, and are established to protect and maintain individual rights.

2.1. Victims' bill of rights

Section 2.1. (A) To preserve and protect victims' rights to justice and due process, a victim of crime has a right:

1. To be treated with fairness, respect, and dignity, and to be free from intimidation, harassment, or abuse, throughout the criminal justice process.

2. To be informed, upon request, when the accused or convicted person is released from custody or has escaped.

3. To be present at and, upon request, to be informed of all criminal proceedings where the defendant has the right to be present.

4. To be heard at any proceeding involving a post-arrest release decision, a negotiated plea, and sentencing.

5. To refuse an interview, deposition, or other discovery request by the defendant, the defendant's attorney, or other person acting on behalf of the defendant.

6. To confer with the prosecution, after the crime against the victim has been charged, before trial or before any disposition of the case and to be informed of the disposition.

7. To read pre-sentence reports relating to the crime against the victim when they are available to the defendant.

8. To receive prompt restitution from the person or persons convicted of the criminal conduct that caused the victim's loss or injury.

9. To be heard at any proceeding when any post-conviction release from confinement is being considered.

10. To a speedy trial or disposition and prompt and final conclusion of the case after the conviction and sentence.

11. To have all rules governing criminal procedure and the admissibility of evidence in all criminal proceedings protect victims' rights and to have these rules be subject to amendment or repeal by the legislature to ensure the protection of these rights.

12. To be informed of victims' constitutional rights.

(B) A victim's exercise of any right granted by this section shall not be grounds for dismissing any criminal proceeding or setting aside any conviction or sentence.

(C) "Victim" means a person against whom the criminal offense has been committed or, if the person is killed or incapacitated, the person's spouse, parent, child or other lawful representative, except if the person is in custody for an offense or is the accused.

(D) The legislature, or the people by initiative or referendum, have the authority to enact substantive and procedural laws to define, implement, preserve and protect the rights guaranteed to victims by this section, including the authority to extend any of these rights to juvenile proceedings.

(E) The enumeration in the constitution of certain rights for victims shall not be construed to deny or disparage others granted by the legislature or retained by victims.

3. Supreme law of the land

Section 3. The Constitution of the United States is the supreme law of the land.

4. Due process of law

Section 4. No person shall be deprived of life, liberty, or property without due process of law.

5. Right of petition and of assembly

Section 5. The right of petition, and of the people peaceably to assemble for the common good, shall never be abridged.

6. Freedom of speech and press

Section 6. Every person may freely speak, write, and publish on all subjects, being responsible for the abuse of that right.

7. Oaths and affirmations

Section 7. The mode of administering an oath, or affirmation, shall be such as shall be most consistent with and binding upon the conscience of the person to whom such oath, or affirmation, may be administered.

8. Right to privacy

Section 8. No person shall be disturbed in his private affairs, or his home invaded, without authority of law.

9. Irrevocable grants of privileges, franchises or immunities

Section 9. No law granting irrevocably any privilege, franchise, or immunity shall be enacted.

10. Self-incrimination; double jeopardy

Section 10. No person shall be compelled in any criminal case to give evidence against himself, or be twice put in jeopardy for the same offense.

11. Administration of justice

Section 11. Justice in all cases shall be administered openly, and without unnecessary delay.

12. Liberty of conscience; appropriations for religious purposes prohibited; religious freedom

Section 12. The liberty of conscience secured by the provisions of this constitution shall not be so construed as to excuse acts of licentiousness, or justify practices inconsistent with the peace and safety of the state. No public money or property shall be appropriated for or applied to any religious worship, exercise, or instruction, or to the support of any religious establishment. No religious qualification shall be required for any public office or employment, nor shall any person be incompetent as a witness or juror in consequence of his opinion on matters of religion, nor be questioned touching his religious belief in any court of justice to affect the weight of his testimony.

13. Equal privileges and immunities

Section 13. No law shall be enacted granting to any citizen, class of citizens, or corporation other than municipal, privileges or immunities which, upon the same terms, shall not equally belong to all citizens or corporations.

14. Habeas corpus

Section 14. The privilege of the writ of habeas corpus shall not be suspended by the authorities of the state.

15. Excessive bail; cruel and unusual punishment

Section 15. Excessive bail shall not be required, nor excessive fines imposed, nor cruel and unusual punishment inflicted.

16. Corruption of blood; forfeiture of estate

Section 16. No conviction shall work corruption of blood, or forfeiture of estate.

17. Eminent domain; just compensation for private property taken; public use as judicial question

Section 17. Private property shall not be taken for private use, except for private ways of necessity, and for drains, flumes, or ditches, on or across the lands of others for mining, agricultural, domestic, or sanitary purposes. No private property shall be taken or damaged for public or private use without just compensation having first been made, paid into court for the owner, secured by bond as may be fixed by the court, or paid into the state treasury for the owner on such terms and conditions as the legislature may provide, and no right of way shall be appropriated to the use of any corporation other than municipal, until full compensation therefore be first made in money, or ascertained and paid into court for the owner, irrespective of any benefit from any improvement proposed by such corporation, which compensation shall be ascertained by a jury, unless a jury be waived as in other civil cases in courts of record, in the manner prescribed by law. Whenever an attempt is made to take private property for a use alleged to be public, the question whether the contemplated use be really public shall be a judicial question, and determined as such without regard to any legislative assertion that the use is public.

18. Imprisonment for debt

Section 18. There shall be no imprisonment for debt, except in cases of fraud.

19. Bribery or illegal rebating; witnesses; self-incrimination no defense

Section 19. Any person having knowledge or possession of facts that tend to establish the guilt of any other person or corporation charged with bribery or illegal rebating, shall not be excused from giving testimony or producing evidence, when legally called upon to do so, on the ground that it may tend to incriminate him under the laws of the state; but no person shall be prosecuted or subject to any penalty or forfeiture for, or on account of, any transaction, matter, or thing concerning which he may so testify or produce evidence.

20. Military power subordinate to civil power

Section 20. The military shall be in strict subordination to the civil power.

21. Free and equal elections

Section 21. All elections shall be free and equal, and no power, civil or military, shall at any time interfere to prevent the free exercise of the right of suffrage.

22. Bailable offenses

Section 22. A. All persons charged with crime shall be bailable by sufficient sureties, except for:

1. Capital offenses, sexual assault, sexual conduct with a minor under fifteen years of age or molestation of a child under fifteen years of age when the proof is evident or the presumption great.

2. Felony offenses committed when the person charged is already admitted to bail on a separate felony charge and where the proof is evident or the presumption great as to the present charge.

3. Felony offenses if the person charged poses a substantial danger to any other person or the community, if no conditions of release which may be imposed will reasonably assure the safety of the other person or the community and if the proof is evident or the presumption great as to the present charge.

B. The purposes of bail and any conditions of release that are set by a judicial officer include:

1. Assuring the appearance of the accused.

2. Protecting against the intimidation of witnesses.

3. Protecting the safety of the victim, any other person or the community.

23. Trial by jury; number of jurors specified by law

Section 23. The right of trial by jury shall remain inviolate. Juries in criminal cases in which a sentence of death or imprisonment for thirty years or more is authorized by law shall consist of twelve persons. In all criminal cases the unanimous consent of the jurors shall be necessary to render a verdict. In all other cases, the number of jurors, not less than six, and the number required to render a verdict, shall be specified by law.

24. Rights of accused in criminal prosecutions

Section 24. In criminal prosecutions, the accused shall have the right to appear and defend in person, and by counsel, to demand the nature and cause of the accusation against him, to have a copy thereof, to testify in his own behalf, to meet the witnesses against him face to face, to have compulsory process to compel the attendance of witnesses in his own behalf, to have a speedy public trial by an impartial jury of the county in which the offense is alleged to have been committed, and the right to appeal in all cases; and in no instance shall any accused person before final judgment be compelled to advance money or fees to secure the rights herein guaranteed.

25. Bills of attainder; ex post facto laws; impairment of contract obligations

Section 25. No bill of attainder, ex-post-facto law, or law impairing the obligation of a contract, shall ever be enacted.

26. Bearing arms

Section 26. The right of the individual citizen to bear arms in defense of himself or the state shall not be impaired, but nothing in this section shall be construed as authorizing individuals or corporations to organize, maintain, or employ an armed body of men.

27. Standing army; quartering soldiers

Section 27. No standing army shall be kept up by this state in time of peace, and no soldier shall in time of peace be quartered in any house without the consent of its owner, nor in time of war except in the manner prescribed by law.

28. Treason

Section 28. Treason against the state shall consist only in levying war against the state, or adhering to its enemies, or in giving them aid and comfort. No person shall be convicted of treason unless on the testimony of two witnesses to the same overt act, or confession in open court.

29. Hereditary emoluments, privileges or powers; perpetuities or entailments

Section 29. No hereditary emoluments, privileges, or powers shall be granted or conferred, and no law shall be enacted permitting any perpetuity or entailment in this state.

30. Indictment or information; preliminary examination

Section 30. No person shall be prosecuted criminally in any court of record for felony or misdemeanor, otherwise than by information or indictment; no person shall be prosecuted for felony by information without having had a preliminary examination before a magistrate or having waived such preliminary examination.

31. Damages for death or personal injuries

Section 31. No law shall be enacted in this state limiting the amount of damages to be recovered for causing the death or injury of any person.

32. Constitutional provisions mandatory

Section 32. The provisions of this Constitution are mandatory, unless by express words they are declared to be otherwise.

33. Reservation of rights

Section 33. The enumeration in this Constitution of certain rights shall not be construed to deny others retained by the people.

34. Industrial pursuits by state and municipal corporations

Section 34. The state of Arizona and each municipal corporation within the state of Arizona shall have the right to engage in industrial pursuits.

Article III

DISTRIBUTION OF POWERS

The powers of the government of the state of Arizona v shall be divided into three separate departments, the legislative, the executive, and the judicial; and, except as provided in this constitution, such departments shall be separate and distinct, and no one of such departments shall exercise the powers properly belonging to either of the others.

Article IV

LEGISLATIVE DEPARTMENT

1. <u>Legislative authority; initiative and referendum</u>

Section 1. (1) Senate; house of representatives; reservation of power to people. The legislative authority of the state shall be vested in the legislature, consisting of a senate and a house of representatives, but the people reserve the power to propose laws and amendments to the constitution and to enact or reject such laws and amendments at the polls, independently of the legislature; and they also reserve, for use at their own option, the power to approve or reject at the polls any act, or item, section, or part of any act, of the legislature.

(2) Initiative power. The first of these reserved powers is the initiative. Under this power ten per centum of the qualified electors shall have the right to propose any measure, and fifteen per centum shall have the right to propose any amendment to the constitution.

(3) Referendum power; emergency measures; effective date of acts. The second of these reserved powers is the referendum. Under this power the legislature, or five per centum of the qualified electors, may order the submission to the people at the polls of any measure, or item, section, or part of any measure, enacted by the legislature, except laws immediately necessary for the preservation of the public peace, health, or safety, or for the support and maintenance of the departments of the state government and state institutions; but to allow opportunity for referendum petitions, no act passed by the legislature shall be operative for ninety days after the close of the session of the legislature enacting such measure, except such as require earlier operation to preserve the public peace, health, or safety, or to provide appropriations for the support and maintenance of the departments of the state and of state institutions; provided, that no such emergency measure shall be considered passed by the legislature unless it shall state in a separate section why it is necessary that it shall become immediately operative, and shall be approved by the affirmative votes of two-thirds of the members elected to each house of the legislature, taken by roll call of ayes and nays, and also approved by the governor; and should such measure be vetoed by the governor, it shall not become a law unless it shall be approved by the votes of three-fourths of the members elected to each house of the legislature, taken by roll call of ayes and nays.

(4) Initiative and referendum petitions; filing. All petitions submitted under the power of the initiative shall be known as initiative petitions, and shall be filed with the secretary of state not less than four months preceding the date of the election at which the measures so proposed are to be voted upon. All petitions submitted under the power of the referendum shall be known as referendum petitions, and shall be filed with the secretary of state not more than ninety days after the final adjournment of the session of the legislature which shall have passed the measure to which the referendum is applied. The filing of a referendum petition against any item, section, or part of any measure shall not prevent the remainder of such measure from becoming operative.

(5) Effective date of initiative and referendum measures. Any measure or amendment to the constitution proposed under the initiative, and any measure to which the referendum is applied, shall be referred to a vote of the qualified electors, and shall become law when approved by a majority of the votes cast thereon and upon proclamation of the governor, and not otherwise.

(6) (A) Veto of initiative or referendum. The veto power of the governor shall not extend to an initiative measure approved by a majority of the votes cast thereon or to a referendum measure decided by a majority of the votes cast thereon.

(6) (B) Legislature's power to repeal initiative or referendum. The legislature shall not have the power to repeal an initiative measure approved by a majority of the votes cast thereon or to repeal a referendum measure decided by a majority of the votes cast thereon.

(6) (C) Legislature's power to amend initiative or referendum. The legislature shall not have the power to amend an initiative measure approved by a majority of the votes cast thereon, or to amend a referendum measure decided by a majority of the votes cast thereon, unless the amending legislation furthers the purposes of such measure and at least three-fourths of the members of each house of the legislature, by a roll call of ayes and nays, vote to amend such measure.

(6) (D) Legislature's power to appropriate or divert funds created by initiative or referendum. The legislature shall not have the power to appropriate or divert funds created or allocated to a specific purpose by an initiative measure approved by a majority of the votes cast thereon, or by a referendum measure decided by a majority of the votes cast thereon, unless the appropriation or diversion of funds furthers the purposes of such measure and at least three-fourths of the members of each house of the legislature, by a roll call of ayes and nays, vote to appropriate or divert such funds.

(7) Number of qualified electors. The whole number of votes cast for all candidates for governor at the general election last preceding the filing of any initiative or referendum petition on a state or county measure shall be the basis on which the number of qualified electors required to sign such petition shall be computed.

(8) Local, city, town or county matters. The powers of the initiative and the referendum are hereby further reserved to the qualified electors of every incorporated city, town, and county as to all local, city, town, or county matters on which such incorporated cities, towns, and counties are or shall be empowered by general laws to legislate. Such incorporated cities, towns, and counties may prescribe the manner of exercising said powers within the restrictions of general laws. Under the power of the initiative fifteen per centum of the qualified electors may propose measures on such local, city, town, or county matters, and ten per centum of the electors may propose the referendum on legislation enacted within and by such city, town, or county. Until provided by general law, said cities and towns may prescribe the basis on which said percentages shall be computed.

(9) Form and contents of initiative and of referendum petitions; verification. Every initiative or referendum petition shall be addressed to the secretary of state in the case of petitions for or on state measures, and to the clerk of the board of supervisors, city clerk, or corresponding officer in the case of petitions for or on county, city, or town measures; and shall contain the declaration of each petitioner, for himself, that he is a qualified elector of the state (and in the case of petitions for or on city, town, or county measures, of the city, town, or county affected), his post office address, the street and number, if any, of his residence, and the date on which he signed such petition. Each sheet containing petitioners' signatures shall be attached to a full and correct copy of the title and text of the measure so proposed to be initiated or referred to the people, and every sheet of every such petition containing signatures shall be verified by the affidavit of the person who circulated said sheet or petition, setting forth that each of the names on said sheet was signed in the presence of the affiant and that in the belief of the affiant each signer was a qualified elector of the state, or in the case of a city, town, or county measure, of the city, town, or county affected by the measure so proposed to be initiated or referred to the people.

(10) Official ballot. When any initiative or referendum petition or any measure referred to the people by the legislature shall be filed, in accordance with this section, with the secretary of state, he shall cause to be printed on the official ballot at the next regular general election the title and number of said measure, together with the words "yes" and "no" in such manner that the electors may express at the polls their approval or disapproval of the measure.

(11) Publication of measures. The text of all measures to be submitted shall be published as proposed amendments to the constitution are published, and in submitting such measures and proposed amendments the secretary of state and all other officers shall be guided by the general law until legislation shall be especially provided therefor.

(12) Conflicting measures or constitutional amendments. If two or more conflicting measures or amendments to the constitution shall be approved by the people at the same election, the measure or amendment receiving the greatest number of affirmative votes shall prevail in all particulars as to which there is conflict.

(13) Canvass of votes; proclamation. It shall be the duty of the secretary of state, in the presence of the governor and the chief justice of the supreme court, to canvass the votes for and against each such measure or proposed amendment to the constitution within thirty days after the election, and upon the completion of the canvass the governor shall forthwith issue a proclamation, giving the whole number of votes cast for and against each measure or proposed amendment, and declaring such measures or amendments as are approved by a majority of those voting thereon to be law.

(14) Reservation of legislative power. This section shall not be construed to deprive the legislature of the right to enact any measure except that the legislature shall not have the power to adopt any measure that supersedes, in whole or in part, any initiative measure approved by a majority of the votes cast thereon or any referendum measure decided by a majority of the votes cast thereon unless the superseding measure furthers the purposes of the initiative or referendum measure and at least three-fourths of the members of each house of the legislature, by a roll call of ayes and nays, vote to supersede such initiative or referendum measure.

(15) Legislature's right to refer measure to the people. Nothing in this section shall be construed to deprive or limit the legislature of the right to order the submission to the people at the polls of any measure, item, section, or part of any measure.

(16) Self-executing. This section of the constitution shall be, in all respects, self-executing.

2. Penalty for violation of initiative and referendum provisions

Section 2. The legislature shall provide a penalty for any wilful violation of any of the provisions of the preceding section

1. Senate; house of representatives; members; special session upon petition of members; congressional and legislative boundaries; citizen commissions

Section 1. (1) The senate shall be composed of one member elected from each of the thirty legislative districts established pursuant to this section.

The house of representatives shall be composed of two members elected from each of the thirty legislative districts established pursuant to this section.

(2) Upon the presentation to the governor of a petition bearing the signatures of not less than two-thirds of the members of each house, requesting a special session of the legislature and designating the date of convening, the governor shall promptly call a special session to assemble on the date specified. At a special session so called the subjects which may be considered by the legislature shall not be limited.

(3) By February 28 of each year that ends in one, an independent redistricting commission shall be established to provide for the redistricting of congressional and state legislative districts. The independent redistricting commission shall consist of five members. No more than two members of the independent redistricting commission shall be members of the same political party. Of the first four members appointed, no more than two shall reside in the same county. Each member shall be a registered Arizona voter who has been continuously registered with the same political party or registered as unaffiliated with a political party for three or more years immediately preceding appointment, who is committed to applying the provisions of this section in an honest, independent and impartial fashion and to upholding public confidence in the integrity of the redistricting process. Within the three years previous to appointment, members shall not have been appointed to, elected to, or a candidate for any other public office, including precinct committeeman or committeewoman but not including school board member or officer, and shall not have served as an officer of a political party, or served as a registered paid lobbyist or as an officer of a candidate's campaign committee.

(4) The commission on appellate court appointments shall nominate candidates for appointment to the independent redistricting commission, except that, if a politically balanced commission exists whose members are nominated by the commission on appellate court appointments and whose regular duties relate to the elective process, the commission on appellate court appointments may delegate to such existing commission (hereinafter called the commission on appellate court appointments' designee) the duty of nominating members for the independent redistricting commission, and all other duties assigned to the commission on appellate court appointments in this section.

(5) By January 8 of years ending in one, the commission on appellate court appointments or its designee shall establish a pool of persons who are willing to serve on and are qualified for appointment to the independent redistricting commission. The pool of candidates shall consist of twenty-five nominees, with ten nominees from each of the two largest political parties in Arizona based on party registration, and five who are not registered with either of the two largest political parties in Arizona.

(6) Appointments to the independent redistricting commission shall be made in the order set forth below. No later than January 31 of years ending in one, the highest ranking officer elected by the Arizona house of representatives shall make one appointment to the independent redistricting commission from the pool of nominees, followed by one appointment from the pool made in turn by each of the following: the minority party leader of the Arizona house of representatives, the highest ranking officer elected by the Arizona senate, and the minority party leader of the Arizona senate. Each such official shall have a seven-day period in which to make an appointment. Any official who fails to make an appointment within the specified time period will forfeit the appointment privilege. In the event that there are two or more minority parties within the house or the senate, the leader of the largest minority party by statewide party registration shall make the appointment.

(7) Any vacancy in the above four independent redistricting commission positions remaining as of March 1 of a year ending in one shall be filled from the pool of nominees by the commission on appellate court appointments or its designee. The appointing body shall strive for political balance and fairness.

(8) At a meeting called by the secretary of state, the four independent redistricting commission members shall select by majority vote from the nomination pool a fifth member who shall not be registered with any party already represented on the independent redistricting commission and who shall serve as chair. If the four commissioners fail to appoint a fifth member within fifteen days, the commission on appellate court appointments or its designee, striving for political balance and fairness, shall appoint a fifth member from the nomination pool, who shall serve as chair.

(9) The five commissioners shall then select by majority vote one of their members to serve as vice-chair.

(10) After having been served written notice and provided with an opportunity for a response, a member of the independent redistricting commission may be removed by the governor, with the concurrence of two-thirds of the senate, for substantial neglect of duty, gross misconduct in office, or inability to discharge the duties of office.

(11) If a commissioner or chair does not complete the term of office for any reason, the commission on appellate court appointments or its designee shall nominate a pool of three candidates within the first thirty days after the vacancy occurs. The nominees shall be of the same political party or status as was the member who vacated the office at the time of his or her appointment, and the appointment other than the chair shall be made by the current holder of the office designated to make the original appointment. The appointment of a new chair shall be made by the remaining commissioners. If the appointment of a replacement commissioner or chair is not made within fourteen days following the presentation of the nominees, the commission on appellate court appointments or its designee shall make the appointment, striving for political balance and fairness. The newly appointed commissioner shall serve out the remainder of the original term.

(12) Three commissioners, including the chair or vice-chair, constitute a quorum. Three or more affirmative votes are required for any official action. Where a quorum is present, the independent redistricting commission shall conduct business in meetings open to the public, with 48 or more hour's public notice provided.

(13) A commissioner, during the commissioner's term of office and for three years thereafter, shall be ineligible for Arizona public office or for registration as a paid lobbyist.

(14) The independent redistricting commission shall establish congressional and legislative districts. The commencement of the mapping process for both the congressional and legislative districts shall be the creation of districts of equal population in a grid-like pattern across the state. Adjustments to the grid shall then be made as necessary to accommodate the goals as set forth below:

A. Districts shall comply with the United States Constitution and the United States voting rights act;

B. Congressional districts shall have equal population to the extent practicable, and state legislative districts shall have equal population to the extent practicable;

C. Districts shall be geographically compact and contiguous to the extent practicable;

D. District boundaries shall respect communities of interest to the extent practicable;

E. To the extent practicable, district lines shall use visible geographic features, city, town and county boundaries, and undivided census tracts.

F. To the extent practicable, competitive districts should be favored where to do so would create no significant detriment to the other goals.

(15) Party registration and voting history data shall be excluded from the initial phase of the mapping process but may be used to test maps for compliance with the above goals. The places of residence of incumbents or candidates shall not be identified or considered.

(16) The independent redistricting commission shall advertise a draft map of congressional districts and a draft map of legislative districts to the public for comment, which comment shall be taken for at least thirty days. Either or both bodies of the legislature may act within this period to make recommendations to the independent redistricting commission by memorial or by minority report, which recommendations shall be considered by the independent redistricting commission. The independent redistricting commission shall then establish final district boundaries.

(17) The provisions regarding this section are self-executing. The independent redistricting commission shall certify to the secretary of state the establishment of congressional and legislative districts.

(18) Upon approval of this amendment, the department of administration or its successor shall make adequate office space available for the independent redistricting commission. The treasurer of the state shall make $6,000,000 available for the work of the independent redistricting commission pursuant to the year 2000 census. Unused monies shall be returned to the state's general fund. In years ending in eight or nine after the year 2001, the department of administration or its successor shall submit to the legislature a recommendation for an appropriation for adequate redistricting expenses and shall make available adequate office space for the operation of the independent redistricting commission. The legislature shall make the necessary appropriations by a majority vote.

(19) The independent redistricting commission, with fiscal oversight from the department of administration or its successor, shall have procurement and contracting authority and may hire staff and consultants for the purposes of this section, including legal representation.

(20) The independent redistricting commission shall have standing in legal actions regarding the redistricting plan and the adequacy of resources provided for the operation of the independent redistricting commission. The independent redistricting commission shall have sole authority to determine whether the Arizona attorney general or counsel hired or selected by the independent redistricting commission shall represent the people of Arizona in the legal defense of a redistricting plan.

(21) Members of the independent redistricting commission are eligible for reimbursement of expenses pursuant to law, and a member's residence is deemed to be the member's post of duty for purposes of reimbursement of expenses.

(22) Employees of the department of administration or its successor shall not influence or attempt to influence the district-mapping decisions of the independent redistricting commission.

(23) Each commissioner's duties established by this section expire upon the appointment of the first member of the next redistricting commission. The independent redistricting commission shall not meet or incur expenses after the redistricting plan is completed, except if litigation or any government approval of the plan is pending, or to revise districts if required by court decisions or if the number of congressional or legislative districts is changed.

2. Qualifications of members of legislature

Section 2. No person shall be a member of the Legislature unless he shall be a citizen of the United States at the time of his election, nor unless he shall be at least twenty-five years of age, and shall have been a resident of Arizona at least three years and of the county from which he is elected at least one year before his election.

3. Sessions of legislature; special sessions; limitation of subjects for consideration

Section 3. The sessions of the legislature shall be held annually at the capitol of the state, and shall commence on the second Monday of January of each year. The governor may call a special session, whenever in his judgment it is advisable. In calling a special session, the governor shall specify the subjects to be considered, and at such special session no laws shall be enacted except such as relate to the subjects mentioned in the call.

4. Disqualification for membership in Legislature

Section 4. No person holding any public office of profit or trust under the authority of the United States, or of this state, shall be a member of the legislature; Provided, that appointments in the state militia and the offices of notary public, justice of the peace, United States commissioner, and postmaster of the fourth class, shall not work disqualification for membership within the meaning of this section.

5. Ineligibility of members of legislature to other public offices

Section 5. No member of the legislature, during the term for which he shall have been elected or appointed shall be eligible to hold any other office or be otherwise employed by the state of Arizona or, any county or incorporated city or town thereof. This prohibition shall not extend to the office of school trustee, nor to employment as a teacher or instructor in the public school system.

6. Privilege from arrest; civil process

Section 6. Members of the legislature shall be privileged from arrest in all cases except treason, felony, and breach of the peace, and they shall not be subject to any civil process during the session of the legislature, nor for fifteen days next before the commencement of each session.

7. Freedom of debate

Section 7. No member of the legislature shall be liable in any civil or criminal prosecution for words spoken in debate.

8. Organization; officers; rules of procedure

Section 8. Each house, when assembled, shall choose its own officers, judge of the election and qualification of its own members, and determine its own rules of procedure.

9. Quorum; compelling attendance; adjournment

Section 9. The majority of the members of each house shall constitute a quorum to do business, but a smaller number may meet, adjourn from day to day, and compel the attendance of absent members, in such manner and under such penalties as each house may prescribe. Neither house shall adjourn for more than three days, nor to any place other than that in which it may be sitting, without the consent of the other.

10. Journal of proceedings; roll call

Section 10. Each house shall keep a journal of its proceedings, and at the request of two members the ayes and nays on roll call on any question shall be entered.

11. Disorderly behavior; expulsion of members

Section 11. Each house may punish its members for disorderly behavior, and may, with the concurrence of two-thirds of its members, expel any member.

12. Procedure on bills; approval or disapproval by governor

Section 12. Every bill shall be read by sections on three different days, unless in case of emergency, two-thirds of either house deem it expedient to dispense with this rule. The vote on the final passage of any bill or joint resolution shall be taken by ayes and nays on roll call. Every measure when finally passed shall be presented to the governor for his approval or disapproval.

13. Subject and title of bills

Section 13. Every act shall embrace but one subject and matters properly connected therewith, which subject shall be expressed in the title; but if any subject shall be embraced in an act which shall not be expressed in the title, such act shall be void only as to so much thereof as shall not be embraced in the title.

14. Legislation by reference prohibited

Section 14. No Act or section thereof shall be revised or amended by mere reference to the title of such act, but the act or section as amended shall be set forth and published at full length.

15. Passage of bills by majority; signing of bills

Section 15. A majority of all members elected to each house shall be necessary to pass any bill, and all bills so passed shall be signed by the presiding officer of each house in open session.

6. Right to protest

Section 16. Any member of the legislature shall have the right to protest and have the reasons of his protest entered on the journal.

17. Extra compensation prohibited; increase or decrease of compensation during term of office

Section 17. The legislature shall never grant any extra compensation to any public officer, agent, servant or contractor, after the services shall have been rendered or the contract entered into, nor shall the compensation of any public officer, other than a justice of the peace, be increased or diminished during his term of office; provided, however, that when any legislative increase or decrease in compensation of the members of any court or the clerk thereof, or of any board or commission composed of two or more officers or persons whose respective terms of office are not coterminous, has heretofore or shall hereafter become effective as to any member or clerk of such court, or any member of such board or commission, it shall be effective from such date as to each thereof.

18. Suits against state

Section 18. The legislature shall direct by law in what manner and in what courts suits may be brought against the state.

19. Local or special laws

Section 19. No local or special laws shall be enacted in any of the following cases, that is to say:

1. Granting divorces.

2. Locating or changing county seats.

3. Changing rules of evidence.

4. Changing the law of descent or succession.

5. Regulating the practice of courts of justice.

6. Limitation of civil actions or giving effect to informal or invalid deeds.

7. Punishment of crimes and misdemeanors.

8. Laying out, opening, altering, or vacating roads, plats, streets, alleys, and public squares.

9. Assessment and collection of taxes.

10. Regulating the rate of interest on money.

11. The conduct of elections.

12. Affecting the estates of deceased persons or of minors.

13. Granting to any corporation, association, or individual, any special or exclusive privileges, immunities, or franchises.

14. Remitting fines, penalties, and forfeitures.

15. Changing names of persons or places.

16. Regulating the jurisdiction and duties of justices of the peace.

17. Incorporation of cities, towns, or villages, or amending their charters.

18. Relinquishing any indebtedness, liability, or obligation to this State.

19. Summoning and empanelling of juries.

20. When a general law can be made applicable.

20. Appropriation bills

Section 20. The general appropriation bill shall embrace nothing but appropriations for the different departments of the state, for state institutions, for public schools, and for interest on the public debt. All other appropriations shall be made by separate bills, each embracing but one subject.

21. Term limits of members of state legislature

Section 21. The members of the first legislature shall hold office until the first Monday in January, 1913. The terms of office of the members of succeeding legislatures shall be two years. No state senator shall serve more than four consecutive terms in that office, nor shall any state representative serve more than four consecutive terms in that office. This limitation on the number of terms of consecutive service shall apply to terms of office beginning on or after January 1, 1993. No legislator, after serving the maximum number of terms, which shall include any part of a term served, may serve in the same office until he has been out of office for no less than one full term.

22. Juvenile justice; certain chronic and violent juvenile offenders prosecuted as adults; community alternatives for certain juvenile offenders; public proceedings and records

Section 22. In order to preserve and protect the right of the people to justice and public safety, and to ensure fairness and accountability when juveniles engage in unlawful conduct, the legislature, or the people by initiative or referendum, shall have the authority to enact substantive and procedural laws regarding all proceedings and matters affecting such juveniles. The following rights, duties, and powers shall govern such proceedings and matters:

1. Juveniles 15 years of age or older accused of murder, forcible sexual assault, armed robbery or other violent felony offenses as defined by statute shall be prosecuted as adults. Juveniles 15 years of age or older who are chronic felony offenders as defined by statute shall be prosecuted as adults. Upon conviction all such juveniles shall be subject to the same laws as adults, except as specifically provided by statute and by article 22, section 16 of this constitution. All other juveniles accused of unlawful conduct shall be prosecuted as provided by law. Every juvenile convicted of or found responsible for unlawful conduct shall make prompt restitution to any victims of such conduct for their injury or loss.

2. County attorneys shall have the authority to defer the prosecution of juveniles who are not accused of violent offenses and who are not chronic felony offenders as defined by statute and to establish community-based alternatives for resolving matters involving such juveniles.

3. All proceedings and matters involving juveniles accused of unlawful conduct shall be open to the public and all records of those proceedings shall be public records. Exceptions shall be made only for the protection of the privacy of innocent victims of crime, or when a court of competent jurisdiction finds a clear public interest in confidentiality.

23. <u>Passes and purchase of transportation by public officers; inapplication to national guard</u>

Section 23. It shall not be lawful for any person holding public office in this state to accept or use a pass or to purchase transportation from any railroad or other corporation, other than as such transportation may be purchased by the general public; Provided, that this shall not apply to members of the national guard of Arizona traveling under orders. The legislature shall enact laws to enforce this provision.

24. <u>Enacting clause of bills; initiative bills</u>

Section 24. The enacting clause of every bill enacted by the legislature shall be as follows: "Be it enacted by the Legislature of the State of Arizona," or when the initiative is used: "Be it enacted by the People of the State of Arizona."

25. <u>Continuity of governmental operations in emergency</u>

Section 25. The legislature, in order to insure continuity of state and local governmental operations in periods of emergency resulting from disasters caused by enemy attack, shall have the power and the immediate duty to:

1. Provide for prompt and temporary succession to the powers and duties of public offices, of whatever nature and whether filled by election or appointment, the incumbents of which may become unavailable for carrying on the powers and duties of such offices.

2. Adopt such other measures as may be necessary and proper for insuring the continuity of governmental operations.

   In the exercise of the powers hereby conferred, the legislature shall in all respects conform to the requirements of this constitution except to the extent that in the judgment of the legislature so to do would be impracticable or would admit of undue delay.

Article V

EXECUTIVE DEPARTMENT

1. <u>Executive department; state officers; terms; election; residence and office at seat of government; duties</u>

(Version amended by 1992 Proposition 100)

Section 1. A. The executive department shall consist of the governor, secretary of state, state treasurer, attorney general, and superintendent of public instruction, each of whom shall hold office for four years beginning on the first Monday of January, 1971 next after the regular general election in 1970.

B. The person having the highest number of the votes cast for the office voted for shall be elected, but if two or more persons have an equal and the highest number of votes for the office, the two houses of the legislature at its next regular session shall elect forthwith, by joint ballot, one of such persons for said office.

C. The officers of the executive department during their terms of office shall reside at the seat of government where they shall keep their offices and the public records, books, and papers. They shall perform such duties as are prescribed by the constitution and as may be provided by law.

1. <u>Term limits on executive department and state officers; term lengths; election; residence and office at seat of government; duties</u>

(Version amended by 1992 Proposition 107)

Section 1. A. The executive department shall consist of the governor, secretary of state, state treasurer, attorney general, and superintendent of public instruction, each of whom shall hold office for a term of four years beginning on the first Monday of January, 1971 next after the regular general election in 1970. No member of the executive department shall hold that office for more than two consecutive terms. This limitation on the number of terms of consecutive service shall apply to terms of office beginning on or after January 1, 1993. No member of the executive department after serving the maximum number of terms, which shall include any part of a term served, may serve in the same office until out of office for no less than one full term.

B. The person having a majority of the votes cast for the office voted for shall be elected. If no person receives a majority of the votes cast for the office, a second election shall be held as prescribed by law between the persons receiving the highest and second highest number of votes cast for the office. The person receiving the highest number of votes at the second election for the office is elected, but if the two persons have an equal number of votes for the office, the two houses of the legislature at its next regular session shall elect forthwith, by joint ballot, one of such persons for said office.

C. The officers of the executive department during their terms of office shall reside at the seat of government where they shall keep their offices and the public records, books, and papers. They shall perform such duties as are prescribed by the constitution and as may be provided by law.

2. Eligibility to state offices

Section 2. No person shall be eligible to any of the offices mentioned in section 1 of this article except a person of the age of not less than twenty-five years, who shall have been for ten years next preceding his election a citizen of the United States, and for five years n3. Governor, commander-in-chief of the military forces

Section 3. The governor shall be commander-in-chief of the military forces of the state, except when such forces shall be called into the service of the United States.

4. Governor; powers and duties; special sessions of legislature; message and recommendations

Section 4. The governor shall transact all executive business with the officers of the government, civil and military, and may require information in writing from the officers in the executive department upon any subject relating to the duties of their respective offices. He shall take care that the laws be faithfully executed. He may convene the legislature in extraordinary session. He shall communicate, by message, to the legislature at every session the condition of the state, and recommend such matters as he shall deem expedient.

5. Reprieves, commutations and pardons

Section 5. The governor shall have power to grant reprieves, commutation, and pardons, after convictions, for all offenses except treason and cases of impeachment, upon such conditions and with such restrictions and limitations as may be provided by law.

6. Death, resignation, removal or disability of governor; succession to office; impeachment, absence from state or temporary disability

Section 6. In the event of the death of the governor, or his resignation, removal from office, or permanent disability to discharge the duties of the office, the secretary of state, if holding by election, shall succeed to the office of governor until his successor shall be elected and shall qualify. If the secretary of state be holding otherwise than by election, or shall fail to qualify as governor, the attorney general, the state treasurer, or the superintendent of public instruction, if holding by election, shall, in the order named, succeed to the office of governor. The taking of the oath of office as governor by any person specified in this section shall constitute resignation from the office by virtue of the holding of which he qualifies as governor. Any successor to the office shall become governor in fact and entitled to all of the emoluments, powers and duties of governor upon taking the oath of office.

In the event of the impeachment of the governor, his absence from the state, or other temporary disability to discharge the duties of the office, the powers and duties of the office of governor shall devolve upon the same person as in case of vacancy, but only until the disability ceases.

7. Presentation of bills to governor; approval; veto; filing with secretary of state; veto of items in appropriation bills; inapplication of veto power to referred bills

Section 7. Every bill passed by the legislature, before it becomes a law, shall be presented to the governor. If he approve, he shall sign it, and it shall become a law as provided in this constitution. But if he disapprove, he shall return it, with his objections, to the house in which it originated, which shall enter the objections at large on the journal. If after reconsideration it again passes both houses by an aye and nay vote on roll call of two-thirds of the members elected to each house, it shall become a law as provided in this constitution, notwithstanding the governor's objections. This section shall not apply to emergency measures as referred to in section 1 of the article on the legislative department.

If any bill be not returned within five days after it shall have been presented to the governor (Sunday excepted) such bill shall become a law in like manner as if he had signed it, unless the legislature by its final adjournment prevents its return, in which case it shall be filed with his objections in the office of the secretary of state within ten days after such adjournment (Sundays excepted) or become a law as provided in this constitution. After the final action by the governor, or following the adoption of a bill notwithstanding his objection, it shall be filed with the secretary of state.

If any bill presented to the governor contains several items of appropriations of money, he may object to one or more of such items, while approving other portions of the bill. In such case he shall append to the bill at the time of signing it, a statement of the item or items which he declines to approve, together with his reasons therefor, and such item or items shall not take effect unless passed over the governor's objections as in this section provided.

The veto power of the governor shall not extend to any bill passed by the legislature and referred to the people for adoption or rejection.

8. Vacancies in office

Section 8. When any office shall, from any cause, become vacant, and no mode shall be provided by the Constitution or by law for filling such vacancy, the governor shall have the power to fill such vacancy by appointment.

9. Powers and duties of state officers

Section 9. The powers and duties of secretary of state, state treasurer, attorney-general, and superintendent of public instruction shall be as prescribed by law.

Canvass of election returns for state officers; certificates of election

Section 10. The returns of the election for all state officers shall be canvassed, and certificates of election issued by the secretary of state, in such manner as may be provided by law.

11. Commissions

Section 11. All commissions shall issue in the name of the state, and shall be signed by the governor, sealed with the seal of the state, and attested by the secretary of state.

12. Compensation of elective state officers; commission on salaries for elective state officers

Section 13. The salaries of those holding elective state offices shall be as established by law from time to time, subject to the limitations of article 6, section 33 and to the limitations of article 4, part 2, section 17. Such salaries as are presently established may be altered from time to time by the procedure established in this section or as otherwise provided by law, except that legislative salaries may be altered only by the procedures established in this section.

A commission to be known as the commission on salaries for elective state officers is authorized to be established by the legislature. The commission shall be composed of five members appointed from private life, two of whom shall be appointed by the governor and one each by the president of the senate, the speaker of the house of representatives, and the chief justice. At such times as may be directed by the legislature, the commission shall report to the governor with recommendations concerning the rates of pay of elected state officers. The governor shall upon the receipt of such report make recommendations to the legislature with respect to the exact rates of pay which he deems advisable for those offices and positions other than for the rates of pay of members of the legislature. Such recommendations shall become effective at a time established by the legislature after the transmission of the recommendation of the governor without aid of further legislative action unless, within such period of time, there has been enacted into law a statute which establishes rates of pay other than those proposed by the governor, or unless either house of the legislature specifically disapproves all or part of the governor's recommendation. The recommendations of the governor, unless disapproved or altered within the time provided by law, shall be effective; and any 1971 recommendations shall be effective as to all offices on the first Monday in January of 1973. In case of either a legislative enactment or disapproval by either house, the recommendations shall be effective only insofar as not altered or disapproved. The recommendations of the commission as to legislative salaries shall be certified by it to the secretary of state and the secretary of state shall submit to the qualified electors at the next regular general election the question, "Shall the recommendations of the commission on salaries for elective state officers concerning legislative salaries be accepted? [ ] Yes [ ] No." Such recommendations if approved by the electors shall become effective at the beginning of the next regular legislative session without any other authorizing legislation. All recommendations which become effective under this section shall supersede all laws enacted prior to their effective date relating to such salaries.

Article VI

JUDICIAL DEPARTMENTS

Judicial power; courts

Section 1. The judicial power shall be vested in an integrated judicial department consisting of a supreme court, such intermediate appellate courts as may be provided by law, a superior court, such courts inferior to the superior court as may be provided by law, and justice courts.

2. Supreme court; composition; divisions; decisions, transaction of business

Section 2. The supreme court shall consist of not less than five justices. The number of justices may be increased or decreased by law, but the court shall at all times be constituted of at least five justices.

The supreme court shall sit in accordance with rules adopted by it, either in banc or in divisions of not less than three justices, but the court shall not declare any law unconstitutional except when sitting in banc. The decisions of the court shall be in writing and the grounds stated.

The court shall be open at all times, except on nonjudicial days, for the transaction of business.

3. Supreme court; administrative supervision; chief justice

Section 3. The supreme court shall have administrative supervision over all the courts of the state. The chief justice shall be elected by the justices of the supreme court from one of their number for a term of five years, and may be reelected for like terms. The vice chief justice shall be elected by the justices of the supreme court from one of their number for a term determined by the court. A member of the court may resign the office of chief justice or vice chief justice without resigning from the court.

The chief justice, or in his absence or incapacity, the vice chief justice, shall exercise the court's administrative supervision over all the courts of the state. He may assign judges of intermediate appellate courts, superior courts, or courts inferior to the superior court to serve in other courts or counties.

4. Supreme court; term of office

Section 4. Justices of the supreme court shall hold office for a regular term of six years except as provided by this article.

5. Supreme court; jurisdiction; writs; rules; habeas corpus

Section 5. The supreme court shall have:

1. Original jurisdiction of habeas corpus, and quo warranto, mandamus, injunction and other extraordinary writs to state officers.

2. Original and exclusive jurisdiction to hear and determine causes between counties concerning disputed boundaries and surveys thereof or concerning claims of one county against another.

3. Appellate jurisdiction in all actions and proceedings except civil and criminal actions originating in courts not of record, unless the action involves the validity of a tax, impost, assessment, toll, statute or municipal ordinance.

4. Power to issue injunctions and writs of mandamus, review, prohibition, habeas corpus, certiorari, and all other writs necessary and proper to the complete exercise of its appellate and revisory jurisdiction.

5. Power to make rules relative to all procedural matters in any court.

6. Such other jurisdiction as may be provided by law.

Each justice of the supreme court may issue writs of habeas corpus to any part of the state upon petition by or on behalf of a person held in actual custody, and may make such writs returnable before himself, the supreme court, appellate court or superior court, or judge thereof.

6. Supreme court; qualifications of justices

Section 6. A justice of the supreme court shall be a person of good moral character and admitted to the practice of law in and a resident of the state of Arizona for ten years next preceding his taking office.

7. Supreme court; clerk and assistants; administrative director and staff

Section 7. The supreme court shall appoint a clerk of the court and assistants thereto who shall serve at its pleasure, and who shall receive such compensation as may be provided by law.

The supreme court shall appoint an administrative director and staff to serve at its pleasure to assist the chief justice in discharging his administrative duties. The director and staff shall receive such compensation as may be provided by law.

8. Supreme court; publication of opinions

Section 8. Provision shall be made by law for the speedy publication of the opinions of the supreme court, and they shall be free for publication by any person.

9. Intermediate appellate courts

Section 9. The jurisdiction, powers, duties and composition of any intermediate appellate court shall be as provided by law.

10. Superior court; number of judges

Section 10. There shall be in each county at least one judge of the superior court. There shall be in each county such additional judges as may be provided by law, but not exceeding one judge for each thirty thousand inhabitants or majority fraction thereof. The number of inhabitants in a county for purposes of this section may be determined by census enumeration or by such other method as may be provided by law.

11. Superior court; presiding judges; duties

Section 11. There shall be in each county a presiding judge of the superior court. In each county in which there are two or more judges, the supreme court shall appoint one of such judges presiding judge. Presiding judges shall exercise administrative supervision over the superior court and judges thereof in their counties, and shall have such other duties as may be provided by law or by rules of the supreme court.

12. Superior court; term of office

Section 12. A. Judges of the superior court in counties having a population of less than two hundred fifty thousand persons according to the most recent United States census shall be elected by the qualified electors of their counties at the general election. They shall hold office for a regular term of four years except as provided by this section from and after the first Monday in January next succeeding their election, and until their successors are elected and qualify. The names of all candidates for judge of the superior court in such counties shall be placed on the regular ballot without partisan or other designation except the division and title of the office.

B. The governor shall fill any vacancy in such counties by appointing a person to serve until the election and qualification of a successor. At the next succeeding general election following the appointment of a person to fill a vacancy, a judge shall be elected to serve for the remainder of the unexpired term.

Judges of the superior court in counties having a population of two hundred fifty thousand persons or more according to the most recent United States census shall hold office for a regular term of four years except as provided by this article.

13. Superior court; composition; salaries; judgments and proceedings; process

Section 13. The superior courts provided for in this article shall constitute a single court, composed of all the duly elected or appointed judges in each of the counties of the state. The legislature may classify counties for the purpose of fixing salaries of judges or officers of the court.

The judgments, decrees, orders and proceedings of any session of the superior court held by one or more judges shall have the same force and effect as if all the judges of the court had presided.

The process of the court shall extend to all parts of the state.

14. Superior court; original jurisdiction

Section 14. The superior court shall have original jurisdiction of:

1. Cases and proceedings in which exclusive jurisdiction is not vested by law in another court.

2. Cases of equity and at law which involve the title to or possession of real property, or the legality of any tax, impost, assessment, toll or municipal ordinance.

3. Other cases in which the demand or value of property in controversy amounts to one thousand dollars or more, exclusive of interest and costs.

4. Criminal cases amounting to felony, and cases of misdemeanor not otherwise provided for by law.

5. Actions of forcible entry and detainer.

6. Proceedings in insolvency.

7. Actions to prevent or abate nuisance.

8. Matters of probate.

9. Divorce and for annulment of marriage.

10. Naturalization and the issuance of papers therefor.

11. Special cases and proceedings not otherwise provided for, and such other jurisdiction as may be provided by law.

15. Jurisdiction and authority in juvenile proceedings

Section 15. The jurisdiction and authority of the courts of this state in all proceedings and matters affecting juveniles shall be as provided by the legislature or the people by initiative or referendum.

16. Superior court; appellate jurisdiction

Section 16. The superior court shall have appellate jurisdiction in cases arising in justice and other courts inferior to the superior court as may be provided by law.

17. Superior court; conduct of business; trial juries; jury trial; grand juries

Section 17. The superior court shall be open at all times, except on nonjudicial days, for the determination of non-jury civil cases and the transaction of business. For the determination of civil causes and matters in which a jury demand has been entered, and for the trial of criminal causes, a trial jury shall be drawn and summoned from the body of the county, as provided by law. The right of jury trial as provided by this constitution shall remain inviolate, but trial by jury may be waived by the parties in any civil cause or by the parties with the consent of the court in any criminal cause. Grand juries shall be drawn and summoned only by order of the superior court.

18. Superior court; writs

Section 18. The superior court or any judge thereof may issue writs of mandamus, quo warranto, review, certiorari, prohibition, and writs of habeas corpus on petition by or on behalf of a person held in actual custody within the county. Injunctions, attachments, and writs of prohibition and habeas corpus may be issued and served on legal holidays and non-judicial days.

19. Superior court; service of judge in another county

Section 19. A judge of the superior court shall serve in another county at the direction of the chief justice of the supreme court or may serve in another county at the request of the presiding judge of the superior court thereof.

20. Retirement and service of retired justices and judges

Section 20. The legislature shall prescribe by law a plan of retirement for justices and judges of courts of record, including the basis and amount of retirement pay, and requiring except as provided in section 35 of this article, that justices and judges of courts of record be retired upon reaching the age of seventy. Any retired justice or judge of any court of record who is drawing retirement pay may serve as a justice or judge of any court. When serving outside his county of residence, any such retired justice or judge shall receive his necessary traveling and subsistence expenses. A retired judge who is temporarily called back to the active duties of a judge is entitled to receive the same compensation and expenses as other like active judges less any amount received for such period in retirement benefits.

21. Superior court; speedy decisions

Section 21. Every matter submitted to a judge of the superior court for his decision shall be decided within sixty days from the date of submission thereof. The supreme court shall by rule provide for the speedy disposition of all matters not decided within such period.

22. Superior and other courts; qualifications of judges

Section 22. Judges of the superior court, intermediate appellate courts or courts inferior to the superior court having jurisdiction in civil cases of one thousand dollars or more, exclusive of interest and costs, established by law under the provisions of section 1 of this article, shall be at least thirty years of age, of good moral character and admitted to the practice of law in and a resident of the state for five years next preceding their taking office.

23. Superior court; clerk

Section 23. There shall be in each county a clerk of the superior court. The clerk shall be elected by the qualified electors of his county at the general election and shall hold office for a term of four years from and after the first Monday in January next succeeding his election. The clerk shall have such powers and perform such duties as may be provided by law or by rule of the supreme court or superior court. He shall receive such compensation as may be provided by law.

24. Superior court; court commissioners, masters and referees

Section 24. Judges of the superior court may appoint court commissioners, masters and referees in their respective counties, who shall have such powers and perform such duties as may be provided by law or by rule of the supreme court. Court commissioners, masters and referees shall receive such compensation as may be provided by law.

25. Style of process; conduct of prosecutions in name of state

Section 25. The style of process shall be "The State of Arizona", and prosecutions shall be conducted in the name of the state and by its authority.

26. Oath of office

Section 26. Each justice, judge and justice of the peace shall, before entering upon the duties of his office, take and subscribe an oath that he will support the Constitution of the United States and the Constitution of the State of Arizona, and that he will faithfully and impartially discharge the duties of his office to the best of his ability.

The oath of all judges of courts inferior to the superior court and the oath of justices of the peace shall be filed in the office of the county recorder, and the oath of all other.

27. Charge to juries; reversal of causes for technical error

Section 27. Judges shall not charge juries with respect to matters of fact, nor comment thereon, but shall declare the law. No cause shall be reversed for technical error in pleadings or proceedings when upon the whole case it shall appear that substantial justice has been done.

28. Justices and judges; dual office holding; political activity; practice of law

Section 28. Justices and judges of courts of record shall not be eligible for any other public office or for any other public employment during their term of office, except that they may assume another judicial office, and upon qualifying therefor, the office formerly held shall become vacant. No justice or judge of any court of record shall practice law during his continuance in office, nor shall he hold any office in a political party or actively take part in any political campaign other than his own for his reelection or retention in office. Any justice or judge who files nomination papers for an elective office, other than for judge of the superior court or a court of record inferior to the superior court in a county having a population of less than two hundred fifty thousand persons according to the most recent United States census, forfeits his judicial office.

30. Courts of record

Section 30. A. The supreme court, the court of appeals and the superior court shall be courts of record. Other courts of record may be established by law, but justice courts shall not be courts of record.

B. All justices and judges of courts of record, except for judges of the superior court and other courts of record inferior to the superior court in counties having a population of less than two hundred fifty thousand persons according to the most recent United States census, shall be appointed in the manner provided in section 37 of this article.

31. <u>Judges pro tempore</u>

Section 31. A. The legislature may provide for the appointment of members of the bar having the qualifications provided in section 22 of this article as judges pro tempore of courts inferior to the supreme court, except that justices of the peace pro tempore shall have the same qualifications as justices of the peace and do not have to reside in the precinct in which the justice of the peace pro tempore is appointed to serve.

B. When serving, any such person shall have all the judicial powers of a regular elected judge of the court to which the person is appointed. A person so appointed shall receive such compensation as may be provided by law. The population limitation of section 10 of this article shall not apply to the appointment of judges pro tempore of the superior court.

32. <u>Justices of the peace and inferior courts; jurisdiction, powers and duties; terms of office; salaries</u>

Section 32. A. The number of justices of the peace to be elected in precincts shall be as provided by law. Justices of the peace may be police justices of incorporated cities and towns.

B. The jurisdiction, powers and duties of courts inferior to the superior court and of justice courts, and the terms of office of judges of such courts and justices of the peace shall be as provided by law. The legislature may classify counties and precincts for the purpose of fixing salaries of judges of courts inferior to the superior court and of justices of the peace.

C. The civil jurisdiction of courts inferior to the superior court and of justice courts shall not exceed the sum of ten thousand dollars, exclusive of interest and costs. Criminal jurisdiction shall be limited to misdemeanors. The jurisdiction of such courts shall not encroach upon the jurisdiction of courts of record but may be made concurrent therewith, subject to the limitations provided in this section.

33. Change by legislature in number of justices or judges; reduction of salary during term of office

Section 33. No change made by the legislature in the number of justices or judges shall work the removal of any justice or judge from office. The salary of any justice or judge shall not be reduced during the term of office for which he was elected or appointed.

34. Absence of judicial officer from state

Section 34. Any judicial officer except a retired justice or judge who absents himself from the state for more than sixty consecutive days shall be deemed to have forfeited his office, but the governor may extend the leave of absence for such time as reasonable necessity therefor exists.

35. Continuance in office; continued existence of offices; application of prior statute and rules

Section 35. A. All justices, judges, justices of the peace and officers of any court who are holding office as such by election or appointment at the time of the adoption of this section shall serve or continue in office for the respective terms for which they are so elected or for their respective unexpired terms, and until their successors are elected or appointed and qualify or they are retained in office pursuant to section 38 of this article; provided, however, that any justice or judge elected at the general election at which this section is adopted shall serve for the term for which he is so elected. The continued existence of any office heretofore legally established or held shall not be abolished or repealed by the adoption of this article. The statutes and rules relating to the authority, jurisdiction, practice and procedure of courts, judicial officers and offices in force at the time of the adoption of this article and not inconsistent herewith, shall, so far as applicable, apply to and govern such courts, judicial officers and offices until amended or repealed.

B. All judges of the superior court holding office by appointment or retention in counties with a population of two hundred fifty thousand persons or more according to the most recent United States census at the time of the adoption of this amendment to this section shall serve or continue in office for the respective terms for which they were appointed. Upon an incumbent vacating the office of judge of the superior court, whether by failing to file a declaration for retention, by rejection by the qualified electors of the county or resignation, the appointment shall be pursuant to section 37 of this article.

36. Commission on appellate court appointments and terms, appointments and vacancies on commission

Section 36. A. There shall be a nonpartisan commission on appellate court appointments which shall be composed of the chief justice of the supreme court, who shall be chairman, five attorney members, who shall be nominated by the board of governors of the state bar of Arizona and appointed by the governor with the advice and consent of the senate in the manner prescribed by law, and ten nonattorney members who shall be appointed by the governor with the advice and consent of the senate in the manner prescribed by law. At least ninety days prior to a term expiring or within twenty-one days of a vacancy occurring for a nonattorney member on the commission for appellate court appointments, the governor shall appoint a nominating committee of nine members, not more than five of whom may be from the same political party. The makeup of the committee shall, to the extent feasible, reflect the diversity of the population of the state. Members shall not be attorneys and shall not hold any governmental office, elective or appointive, for profit. The committee shall provide public notice that a vacancy exists and shall solicit, review and forward to the governor all applications along with the committee's recommendations for appointment.

Attorney members of the commission shall have resided in the state and shall have been admitted to practice before the supreme court for not less than five years. Not more than three attorney members shall be members of the same political party and not more than two attorney members shall be residents of any one county. Nonattorney members shall have resided in the state for not less than five years and shall not be judges, retired judges or admitted to practice before the supreme court. Not more than five nonattorney members shall be members of the same political party. Not more than two nonattorney members shall be residents of any one county. None of the attorney or nonattorney members of the commission shall hold any governmental office, elective or appointive, for profit, and no attorney member shall be eligible for appointment to any judicial office of the state until one year after he ceases to be a member. Attorney members of the commission shall serve staggered four-year terms and nonattorney members shall serve staggered four-year terms. Vacancies shall be filled for the unexpired terms in the same manner as the original appointments.

B. No person other than the chief justice shall serve at the same time as a member of more than one judicial appointment commission.

C. In making or confirming appointments to the appellate court commission, the governor, the senate and the state bar shall endeavor to see that the commission reflects the diversity of Arizona's population.

In the event of the absence or incapacity of the chairman the supreme court shall appoint a justice thereof to serve in his place and stead.

D. Prior to making recommendations to the governor as hereinafter provided, the commission shall conduct investigations, hold public hearings and take public testimony. An executive session as prescribed by rule may be held upon a two-thirds vote of the members of the commission in a public hearing. Final decisions as to recommendations shall be made without regard to political affiliation in an impartial and objective manner. The commission shall consider the diversity of the state's population, however the primary consideration shall be merit. Voting shall be in a public hearing. The expenses of meetings of the commission and the attendance of members thereof for travel and subsistence shall be paid from the general fund of the state as state officers are paid, upon claims approved by the chairman.

E. After public hearings the supreme court shall adopt rules of procedure for the commission on appellate court appointments.

F. Notwithstanding the provisions of subsection A, the initial appointments for the five additional nonattorney members and the two additional attorney members of the commission shall be designated by the governor for staggered terms as follows:

1. One appointment for a nonattorney member shall be for a one-year term.

2. Two appointments for nonattorney members shall be for a two-year term.

3. Two appointments for nonattorney members shall be for a three-year term.

4. One appointment for an attorney member shall be for a one-year term.

5. One appointments for an attorney member shall be for a two-year term.

G. The members currently serving on the commission may continue to serve until the expiration of their normal terms. All subsequent appointments shall be made as prescribed by this section.

37. <u>Judicial vacancies and appointments; initial terms; residence; age</u>

Section 37. A. Within sixty days from the occurrence of a vacancy in the office of a justice or judge of any court of record, except for vacancies occurring in the office of a judge of the superior court or a judge of a court of record inferior to the superior court, the commission on appellate court appointments, if the vacancy is in the supreme court or an intermediate appellate court of record, shall submit to the governor the names of not less than three persons nominated by it to fill such vacancy, no more than two of whom shall be members of the same political party unless there are more than four such nominees, in which event not more than sixty percentum of such nominees shall be members of the same political party.

B. Within sixty days from the occurrence of a vacancy in the office of a judge of the superior court or a judge of a court of record inferior to the superior court except for vacancies occurring in the office of a judge of the superior court or a judge of a court of record inferior to the superior court in a county having a population of less than two hundred fifty thousand persons according to the most recent United States census, the commission on trial court appointments for the county in which the vacancy occurs shall submit to the governor the names of not less than three persons nominated by it to fill such vacancy, no more than two of whom shall be members of the same political party unless there are more than four such nominees, in which event no more than sixty per centum of such nominees shall be members of the same political party. A nominee shall be under sixty-five years of age at the time his name is submitted to the governor. Judges of the superior court shall be subject to retention or rejection by a vote of the qualified electors of the county from which they were appointed at the general election in the manner provided by section 38 of this article.

C. A vacancy in the office of a justice or a judge of such courts of record shall be filled by appointment by the governor without regard to political affiliation from one of the nominees whose names shall be submitted to him as hereinabove provided. In making the appointment, the governor shall consider the diversity of the state's population for an appellate court appointment and the diversity of the county's population for a trial court appointment, however the primary consideration shall be merit. If the governor does not appoint one of such nominees to fill such vacancy within sixty days after their names are submitted to the governor by such commission, the chief justice of the supreme court forthwith shall appoint on the basis of merit alone without regard to political affiliation one of such nominees to fill such vacancy. If such commission does not, within sixty days after such vacancy occurs, submit the names of nominees as hereinabove provided, the governor shall have the power to appoint any qualified person to fill such vacancy at any time thereafter prior to the time the names of the nominees to fill such vacancy are submitted to the governor as hereinabove provided. Each justice or judge so appointed shall initially hold office for a term ending sixty days following the next regular general election after the expiration of a term of two years in office. Thereafter, the terms of justices or judges of the supreme court and the superior court shall be as provided by this article.

D. A person appointed to fill a vacancy on an intermediate appellate court or another court of record now existing or hereafter established by law shall have been a resident of the counties or county in which that vacancy exists for at least one year prior to his appointment, in addition to possessing the other required qualifications. A nominee shall be under sixty-five years of age at the time his name is submitted to the governor.

38. Declaration of candidacy; form of judicial ballot, rejection and retention; failure to file declaration

Section 38. A. A justice or judge of the supreme court or an intermediate appellate court shall file in the office of the secretary of state, and a judge of the superior court or other court of record including such justices or judges who are holding office as such by election or appointment at the time of the adoption of this section except for judges of the superior court and other courts of record inferior to the superior court in counties having a population of less than two hundred fifty thousand persons, according to the United States census, shall file in the office of the clerk of the board of supervisors of the county in which he regularly sits and resides, not less than sixty nor more than ninety days prior to the regular general election next preceding the expiration of his term of office, a declaration of his desire to be retained in office, and the secretary of state shall certify to the several boards of supervisors the appropriate names of the candidate or candidates appearing on such declarations filed in his office.

B. The name of any justice or judge whose declaration is filed as provided in this section shall be placed on the appropriate official ballot at the next regular general election under a nonpartisan designation and in substantially the following form:

Shall _____, (Name of justice or judge) of the _____ court be retained in office? Yes __ No __ (Mark X after one).

C. If a majority of those voting on the question votes "No," then, upon the expiration of the term for which such justice or judge was serving, a vacancy shall exist, which shall be filled as provided by this article. If a majority of those voting on the question votes "Yes," such justice or judge shall remain in office for another term, subject to removal as provided by this constitution.

D. The votes shall be counted and canvassed and the result declared as in the case of state and county elections, whereupon a certificate of retention or rejection of the incumbent justice or judge shall be delivered to him by the secretary of state or the clerk of the board of supervisors, as the case may be.

E. If a justice or judge fails to file a declaration of his desire to be retained in office, as required by this section, then his office shall become vacant upon expiration of the term for which such justice or judge was serving.

39. Retirement of justices and judges; vacancies

Section 39. On attaining the age of seventy years a justice or judge of a court of record shall retire and his judicial office shall be vacant, except as otherwise provided in section 35 of this article. In addition to becoming vacant as provided in this section, the office of a justice or judge of any court of record becomes vacant upon his death or his voluntary retirement pursuant to statute or his voluntary resignation, and also, as provided in section 38 of this article, upon the expiration of his term next following a general election at which a majority of those voting on the question of his retention vote in the negative or for which general election he is required, but fails, to file a declaration of his desire to be retained in office.

This section is alternative to and cumulative with the methods of removal of judges and justices provided in parts 1 and 2 of article 8 and article 6.1 of this Constitution.

40. Option for counties with less than two hundred fifty thousand persons

Section 40. Notwithstanding any provision of this article to the contrary, any county having a population of less than two hundred fifty thousand persons, according to the most recent United States census, may choose to select its judges of the superior court or of courts of record inferior to the superior court as if it had a population of two hundred fifty thousand or more persons. Such choice shall be determined by vote of the qualified electors of such county voting on the question at an election called for such purpose by resolution of the board of supervisors of such county. If such qualified electors approve, the provisions of sections 12, 28, 30, 35 through 39, 41 and 42 shall apply as if such county had a population of two hundred fifty thousand persons or more.

41. Superior court divisions; commission on trial court appointments; membership; terms

A. Except as otherwise provided, judges of the superior court in counties having a population of two hundred fifty thousand persons or more according to the most recent United States census shall hold office for a regular term of four years.

B. There shall be a nonpartisan commission on trial court appointments for each county having a population of two hundred fifty thousand persons or more according to the most recent United States census which shall be composed of the following members:

1. The chief justice of the supreme court, who shall be the chairman of the commission. In the event of the absence or incapacity of the chairman the supreme court shall appoint a justice thereof to serve in his place and stead.

2. Five attorney members, none of whom shall reside in the same supervisorial district and not more than three of whom shall be members of the same political party, who are nominated by the board of governors of the state bar of Arizona and who are appointed by the governor subject to confirmation by the senate in the manner prescribed by law.

3. Ten nonattorney members, no more than two of whom shall reside in the same supervisorial district.

C. At least ninety days prior to a term expiring or within twenty-one days of a vacancy occurring for a nonattorney member on the commission for trial court appointments, the member of the board of supervisors from the district in which the vacancy has occurred shall appoint a nominating committee of seven members who reside in the district, not more than four of whom may be from the same political party. The make-up of the committee shall, to the extent feasible, reflect the diversity of the population of the district. Members shall not be attorneys and shall not hold any governmental office, elective or appointive, for profit. The committee shall provide public notice that a vacancy exists and shall solicit, review and forward to the governor all applications along with the committee's recommendations for appointment. The governor shall appoint two persons from each supervisorial district who shall not be of the same political party, subject to confirmation by the senate in the manner prescribed by law.

D. In making or confirming appointments to trial court commissions, the governor, the senate and the state bar shall endeavor to see that the commission reflects the diversity of the county's population.

E. Members of the commission shall serve staggered four year terms, except that initial appointments for the five additional nonattorney members and the two additional attorney members of the commission shall be designated by the governor as follows:

1. One appointment for a nonattorney member shall be for a one-year term.

2. Two appointments for nonattorney members shall be for a two-year term.

3. Two appointments for nonattorney members shall be for a three-year term.

4. One appointment for an attorney member shall be for a one-year term.

5. One appointment for an attorney member shall be for a two-year term.

F. Vacancies shall be filled for the unexpired terms in the same manner as the original appointments.

G. Attorney members of the commission shall have resided in this state and shall have been admitted to practice in this state by the supreme court for at least five years and shall have resided in the supervisorial district from which they are appointed for at least one year. Nonattorney members shall have resided in this state for at least five years, shall have resided in the supervisorial district for at least one year before being nominated and shall not be judges, retired judges nor admitted to practice before the supreme court. None of the attorney or nonattorney members of the commission shall hold any governmental office, elective or appointive, for profit and no attorney member is eligible for appointment to any judicial office of this state until one year after membership in the commission terminates.

H. No person other than the chief justice shall serve at the same time as a member of more than one judicial appointment commission.

I. The commission shall submit the names of not less than three individuals for nomination for the office of the superior court judge pursuant to section 37 of this article.

J. Prior to making recommendations to the governor, the commission shall conduct investigations, hold public hearings and take public testimony. An executive session as prescribed by rule may be held upon a two-thirds vote of the members of the commission in a public hearing. Final decisions as to recommendations shall be made without regard to political affiliation in an impartial and objective manner. The commission shall consider the diversity of the county's population and the geographical distribution of the residences of the judges throughout the county, however the primary consideration shall be merit. Voting shall be in a public hearing. The expenses of meetings of the commission and the attendance of members thereof for travel and subsistence shall be paid from the general fund of the state as state officers are paid, upon claims approved by the chairman.

K. After public hearings the supreme court shall adopt rules of procedure for the commission on trial court appointments.

L. The members of the commission who were appointed pursuant to section 36 of this article prior to the effective date of this section may continue to serve until the expiration of their normal terms. All subsequent appointments shall be made as prescribed by this section.

42. Retention evaluation of justices and judges

The supreme court shall adopt, after public hearings, and administer for all justices and judges who file a declaration to be retained in office, a process, established by court rules for evaluating judicial performance. The rules shall include written performance standards and performance reviews which survey opinions of persons who have knowledge of the justice's or judge's performance. The public shall be afforded a full and fair opportunity for participation in the evaluation process through public hearings, dissemination of evaluation reports to voters and any other methods as the court deems advisable.

Article VI.I

COMMISSION ON JUDICIAL CONDUCT

1. Composition; appointment; term; vacancies

Section 1. A. A commission on judicial conduct is created to be composed of eleven persons consisting of two judges of the court of appeals, two judges of the superior court, one justice of the peace and one municipal court judge, who shall be appointed by the supreme court, two members of the state bar of Arizona, who shall be appointed by the governing body of such bar association, and three citizens who are not judges, retired judges nor members of the state bar of Arizona, who shall be appointed by the governor subject to confirmation by the senate in the manner prescribed by law.

B. Terms of members of the commission shall be six years, except that initial terms of two members appointed by the supreme court and one member appointed by the state bar of Arizona for terms which begin in January, 1991 shall be for two years and initial terms of one member appointed by the supreme court and one member appointed by the state bar of Arizona for terms which begin in January, 1991 shall be for four years. If a member ceases to hold the position that qualified him for appointment his membership on the commission terminates. An appointment to fill a vacancy for an unexpired term shall be made for the remainder of the term by the appointing power of the original appointment.

2. Disqualification of judge

Section 2. A judge is disqualified from acting as a judge, without loss of salary, while there is pending an indictment or an information charging him in the United States with a crime punishable as a felony under Arizona or federal law, or a recommendation to the supreme court by the commission on judicial conduct for his suspension, removal or retirement.

3. Suspension or removal of judge

Section 3. On recommendation of the commission on judicial conduct, or on its own motion, the supreme court may suspend a judge from office without salary when, in the United States, he pleads guilty or no contest or is found guilty of a crime punishable as a felony under Arizona or federal law or of any other crime that involves moral turpitude under such law. If his conviction is reversed the suspension terminates, and he shall be paid his salary for the period of suspension. If he is suspended and his conviction becomes final the supreme court shall remove him from office.

4. Retirement of judge

Section 4. On recommendation of the commission on judicial conduct, the supreme court may retire a judge for disability that seriously interferes with the performance of his duties and is or is likely to become permanent, and may censure, suspend without pay or remove a judge for action by him that constitutes wilful misconduct in office, wilful and persistent failure to perform his duties, habitual intemperance or conduct prejudicial to the administration of justice that brings the judicial office into disrepute.

B. A judge retired by the supreme court shall be considered to have retired voluntarily. A judge removed by the supreme court is ineligible for judicial office in this state.

5. Definitions and rules implementing article

Section 5. The term "judge" as used in this article shall apply to all justices of the peace, judges in courts inferior to the superior court as may be provided by law, judges of the superior court, judges of the court of appeals and justices of the supreme court. The supreme court shall make rules implementing this article and providing for confidentiality of proceedings. A judge who is a member of the commission or supreme court shall not participate as a member in any proceedings hereunder involving his own censure, suspension, removal or involuntary retirement.

6. Article self-executing

Section 6. The provisions of this article shall be self-executing.

Article VII

SUFFRAGE AND ELECTIONS

1. Method of voting; secrecy

Section 1. All elections by the people shall be by ballot, or by such other method as may 2. Qualifications of voters; disqualification

Section 2. A. No person shall be entitled to vote at any general election, or for any office that now is, or hereafter may be, elective by the people, or upon any question which may be submitted to a vote of the people, unless such person be a citizen of the United States of the age of eighteen years or over, and shall have resided in the state for the period of time preceding such election as prescribed by law, provided that qualifications for voters at a general election for the purpose of electing presidential electors shall be as prescribed by law. The word "citizen" shall include persons of the male and female sex.

B. The rights of citizens of the United States to vote and hold office shall not be denied or abridged by the state, or any political division or municipality thereof, on account of sex, and the right to register, to vote and to hold office under any law now in effect, or which may hereafter be enacted, is hereby extended to, and conferred upon males and females alike.

C. No person who is adjudicated an incapacitated person shall be qualified to vote at any election, nor shall any person convicted of treason or felony, be qualified to vote at any election unless restored to civil rights

3. Voting residence of federal employees and certain others

Section 3. For the purpose of voting, no person shall be deemed to have gained or lost a residence by reason of being present or absent while employed in the service of the United States, or while a student at any institution of learning, or while kept at any institution or other shelter at public expense, or while confined in any public jail or prison.

4. Privilege of electors from arrest

Section 4. Electors shall in all cases, except treason, felony, or breach of the peace, be privileged from arrest during their attendance at any election, and in going thereto and returning therefrom.

5. Military duty on day of election

Section 5. No elector shall be obliged to perform military duty on the day of an election, except in time of war or public danger.

6. Residence of military personnel stationed within state

Section 6. No soldier, seaman, or marine, in the army or navy of the United States shall be deemed a resident of this state in consequence of his being stationed at any military or naval place within this state.

7. Highest number of votes received as determinative of person elected

Section 7. In all elections held by the people in this state, the person, or persons, receiving the highest number of legal votes shall be declared elected.

8. Qualifications for voters at school elections

Section 8. Qualifications for voters at school elections shall be as are now, or as may hereafter be, provided by law.

9. Advisory vote

Section 9. For the purpose of obtaining an advisory vote of the people, the legislature shall provide for placing the names of candidates for United States senator on the official ballot at the general election next preceding the election of a United States senator.

10. Direct primary election law

Section 10. The Legislature shall enact a direct primary election law, which shall provide for the nomination of candidates for all elective State, county, and city offices, including candidates for United States Senator and for Representative in Congress. Any person who is registered as no party preference or independent as the party preference or who is registered with a political party that is not qualified for representation on the ballot may vote in the primary election of any one of the political parties that is qualified for the ballot.

11. General elections; date

Section 11. There shall be a general election of representatives in congress, and of state, county, and precinct officers on the first Tuesday after the first Monday in November of the first even numbered year after the year in which Arizona is admitted to statehood and biennially thereafter.

12. Registration and other laws

Section 12. There shall be enacted registration and other laws to secure the purity of elections and guard against abuses of the elective franchise.

13. Submission of questions upon bond issues or special assessments

Section 13. Questions upon bond issues or special assessments shall be submitted to the vote of real property tax payers, who shall also in all respects be qualified electors of this State, and of the political subdivisions thereof affected by such question.

14. Fee for placing candidate's name on ballot

Section 14. No fee shall ever be required in order to have the name of any candidate placed on the official ballot for any election or primary.

15. Qualifications for public office

Section 15. Every person elected or appointed to any elective office of trust or profit under the authority of the state, or any political division or any municipality thereof, shall be a qualified elector of the political division or municipality in which such person shall be elected.

16. Campaign contributions and expenditures; publicity

Section 16. The legislature, at its first session, shall enact a law providing for a general publicity, before and after election, of all campaign contributions to, and expenditures of campaign committees and candidates for public office.

17. Vacancy in Congress

Section 17. There shall be a primary and general election as prescribed by law, which shall provide for nomination and election of a candidate for United States senator and for representative in congress when a vacancy occurs through resignation or any other cause.

18. Term limits on ballot appearances in congressional elections.

Section 18. The name of any candidate for United States senator from Arizona shall not appear on the ballot if, by the end of the current term of office, the candidate will have served (or, but for resignation, would have served) in that office for two consecutive terms, and the name of a candidate for United States representative from Arizona shall not appear on the ballot if, by the end of the current term of office, the candidate will have served (or, but for resignation, would have served) in that office for three consecutive terms. Terms are considered consecutive unless they are at least one full term apart. Any person appointed or elected to fill a vacancy in the United States congress who serves at least one half of a term of office shall be considered to have served a term in that office for purposes of this section. For purposes of this section, terms beginning before January 1, 1993 shall not be considered.

Article VIII

REMOVAL FROM OFFICE

1. Officers subject to recall; petitioners

Section 1. Every public officer in the state of Arizona, holding an elective office, either by election or appointment, is subject to recall from such office by the qualified electors of the electoral district from which candidates are elected to such office. Such electoral district may include the whole state. Such number of said electors as shall equal twenty-five per centum of the number of votes cast at the last preceding general election for all of the candidates for the office held by such officer, may by petition, which shall be known as a recall petition, demand his recall.

2. Recall petitions; contents; filing; signatures; oath

Section 2. Every recall petition must contain a general statement, in not more than two hundred words, of the grounds of such demand, and must be filed in the office in which petitions for nominations to the office held by the incumbent are required to be filed. The signatures to such recall petition need not all be on one sheet of paper, but each signer must add to his signature the date of his signing said petition, and his place of residence, giving his street and number, if any, should he reside in a town or city. One of the signers of each sheet of such petition, or the person circulating such sheet, must make and subscribe an oath on said sheet, that the signatures thereon are genuine.

3. Resignation of officer; special election

Section 3. If such officer shall offer his resignation it shall be accepted, and the vacancy shall be filled as may be provided by law. If he shall not resign within five days after a recall petition is filed as provided by law, a special election shall be ordered to be held as provided by law, to determine whether such officer shall be recalled. On the ballots at such election shall be printed the reasons as set forth in the petition for demanding his recall, and, in not more than two hundred words, the officer's justification of his course in office. He shall continue to perform the duties of his office until the result of such election shall have been officially declared.

4. Special election; candidates; results; qualification of successor

Section 4. Unless the incumbent otherwise requests, in writing, the incumbent's name shall be placed as a candidate on the official ballot without nomination. Other candidates for the office may be nominated to be voted for at said election. The candidate who receives the highest number of votes shall be declared elected for the remainder of the term. Unless the incumbent receives the highest number of votes, the incumbent shall be deemed to be removed from office, upon qualification of the successor. In the event that the successor shall not qualify within five days after the result of said election shall have been declared, the said office shall be vacant, and may be filled as provided by law.

5. Recall petitions; restrictions and conditions

Section 5. No recall petition shall be circulated against any officer until he shall have held his office for a period of six months, except that it may be filed against a member of the legislature at any time after five days from the beginning of the first session after his election. After one recall petition and election, no further recall petition shall be filed against the same officer during the term for which he was elected, unless petitioners signing such petition shall first pay into the public treasury which has paid such election expenses, all expenses of the preceding election.

6. Application of general election laws; implementary legislation

Section 6. The general election laws shall apply to recall elections in so far as applicable. Laws necessary to facilitate the operation of the provisions of this article shall be enacted, including provision for payment by the public treasury of the reasonable special election campaign expenses of such officer.

Part 2 1. Power of impeachment in house of representatives; trial by senate

Section 1. The house of representatives shall have the sole power of impeachment. The concurrence of a majority of all the members shall be necessary to an impeachment. All impeachments shall be tried by the senate, and, when sitting for that purpose, the senators shall be upon oath or affirmation to do justice according to law and evidence, and shall be presided over by the chief justice of the supreme court. Should the chief justice be on trial, or otherwise disqualified, the senate shall elect a judge of the supreme court to preside.

2. Conviction; grounds for impeachment; judgment; liability to trial

Section 2. No person shall be convicted without a concurrence of two-thirds of the senators elected. The governor and other state and judicial officers, except justices of courts not of record, shall be liable to impeachment for high crimes, misdemeanors, or malfeasance in office, but judgment in such cases shall extend only to removal from office and disqualification to hold any office of honor, trust, or profit in the state. The party, whether convicted or acquitted, shall, nevertheless, be liable to trial and punishment according to law.

Article IX

PUBLIC DEBT, REVENUE AND TAXATION

1. Surrender of power of taxation; uniformity of taxes

Section 1. The power of taxation shall never be surrendered, suspended or contracted away. Except as provided by section 18 of this article, all taxes shall be uniform upon the same class of property within the territorial limits of the authority levying the tax, and shall be levied and collected for public purposes only.

2. Property subject to taxation; exemptions

Section 2. (1) There shall be exempt from taxation all federal, state, county and municipal property.

(2) Property of educational, charitable and religious associations or institutions not used or held for profit may be exempt from taxation by law.

(3) Public debts, as evidenced by the bonds of Arizona, its counties, municipalities or other subdivisions, shall also be exempt from taxation.

(4) All household goods owned by the user thereof and used solely for noncommercial purposes shall be exempt from taxation, and such person entitled to such exemption shall not be required to take any affirmative action to receive the benefit of such exemption.

(5) Stocks of raw or finished materials, unassembled parts, work in process or finished products constituting the inventory of a retailer or wholesaler located within the state and principally engaged in the resale of such materials, parts or products, whether or not for resale to the ultimate consumer, shall be exempt from taxation.

(6) The legislature may exempt personal property that is used for agricultural purposes or in a trade or business from taxation in a manner provided by law, except that the exemption does not apply to any amount of the full cash value of the personal property of a taxpayer that exceeds fifty thousand dollars. The legislature may provide by law to increase the exempt amount according to annual variations in a designated national inflation index.

(7) The legislature may exempt the property of cemeteries that are set apart and used to inter deceased human beings from taxation in a manner provided by law.

(8) There shall be further exempt from taxation the property of each honorably discharged airman, soldier, sailor, United States marine, member of revenue marine service, the coast guard, nurse corps or of any predecessor or of the component of auxiliary of any thereof, resident of this state, in the amount of:

(a) One thousand five hundred dollars if the total assessment of such person does not exceed three thousand five hundred dollars.

(b) One thousand dollars if the total assessment of such person does not exceed four thousand dollars.

(c) Five hundred dollars if the total assessment of such person does not exceed four thousand five hundred dollars.

(d) Two hundred fifty dollars if the total assessment of such person does not exceed five thousand dollars.

(e) No exemption if the total assessment of such person exceeds five thousand dollars.

No such exemption shall be made for such person unless such person shall have served at least sixty days in the military or naval service of the United States during World War I or prior wars and shall have been a resident of this state prior to September 1, 1945.

(9) There shall be further exempt from taxation as herein provided the property of each honorably discharged airman, soldier, sailor, United States marine, member of revenue marine service, the coast guard, nurse corps or of any predecessor or of the component of auxiliary of any thereof, resident of this state, where such person has a service-connected disability as determined by the United States veterans administration or its successor. No such exemption shall be made for such person unless he shall have been a resident of this state prior to September 1, 1945 or unless such person shall have been a resident of this state for at least four years prior to his original entry into service as an airman, soldier, sailor, United States marine, member of revenue marine service, the coast guard, nurse corps or of any predecessor or of the component of auxiliary of any thereof. The property of such person having a compensable service-connected disability exempt from taxation as herein provided shall be determined as follows:

(a) If such person's service-connected disability as determined by the United States veterans administration or its successor is sixty per cent or less, the property of such person exempt from taxation shall be determined by such person's percentage of disability multiplied by the assessment of such person in the amount of:

(i) One thousand five hundred dollars if the total assessment of such person does not exceed three thousand five hundred dollars.

(ii) One thousand dollars if the total assessment of such person does not exceed four thousand dollars.

(iii) Five hundred dollars if the total assessment of such person does not exceed four thousand five hundred dollars.

(iv) Two hundred fifty dollars if the total assessment of such person does not exceed five thousand dollars.

(v) No exemption if the total assessment of such person exceeds five thousand dollars.

(b) If such person's service-connected disability as determined by the United States veterans administration or its successor is more than sixty per cent, the property of such person exempt from taxation shall be in the amount of:

(i) One thousand five hundred dollars if the total assessment of such person does not exceed three thousand five hundred dollars.

(ii) One thousand dollars if the total assessment of such person does not exceed four thousand dollars.

(iii) Five hundred dollars if the total assessment of such person does not exceed four thousand five hundred dollars.

(iv) Two hundred fifty dollars if the total assessment of such person does not exceed five thousand dollars.

(v) No exemption if the total assessment of such person exceeds five thousand dollars.

(10) There shall be further exempt from taxation the property of each honorably discharged airman, soldier, sailor, United States marine, member of revenue marine service, the coast guard, nurse corps or of any predecessor or of the component of auxiliary of any thereof, resident of this state, where such person has a nonservice-connected total and permanent disability, physical or mental, as so certified by the United States veterans administration, or its successor, or such other certification as provided by law, in the amount of:

(a) One thousand five hundred dollars if the total assessment of such person does not exceed three thousand five hundred dollars.

(b) One thousand dollars if the total assessment of such person does not exceed four thousand dollars.

(c) Five hundred dollars if the total assessment of such person does not exceed four thousand five hundred dollars.

(d) Two hundred fifty dollars if the total assessment of such person does not exceed five thousand dollars.

(e) No exemption if the total assessment of such person exceeds five thousand dollars.

No such exemption shall be made for such person unless he shall have served at least sixty days in the military or naval service of the United States during time of war after World War I and shall have been a resident of this state prior to September 1, 1945.

(11) There shall be further exempt from taxation the property of each widow, resident of this state, in the amount of:

(a) One thousand five hundred dollars if the total assessment of such widow does not exceed three thousand five hundred dollars.

(b) One thousand dollars if the total assessment of such widow does not exceed four thousand dollars.

(c) Five hundred dollars if the total assessment of such widow does not exceed four thousand five hundred dollars.

(d) Two hundred fifty dollars if the total assessment of such widow does not exceed five thousand dollars.

(e) No exemption if the total assessment of such widow exceeds five thousand dollars.

In order to qualify for this exemption, the income from all sources of such widow, together with the income from all sources of all children of such widow residing with the widow in her residence in the year immediately preceding the year for which such widow applies for this exemption, shall not exceed:

1. Seven thousand dollars if none of the widow's children under the age of eighteen years resided with her in such widow's residence; or

2. Ten thousand dollars if one or more of the widow's children residing with her in such widow's residence was under the age of eighteen years, or was totally and permanently disabled, physically or mentally, as certified by competent medical authority as provided by law.

   Such widow shall have resided with her last spouse in this state at the time of the spouse's death if she was not a widow and a resident of this state prior to January 1, 1969.

(12) No property shall be exempt which has been conveyed to evade taxation. The total exemption from taxation granted to the property owned by a person who qualifies for any exemption in accordance with the terms of subsections (8), (9), (10) or (11) shall not exceed one thousand five hundred dollars. The provisions of this section shall be self-executing.

(13) All property in the state not exempt under the laws of the United States or under this constitution or exempt by law under the provisions of this section shall be subject to taxation to be ascertained as provided by law.

2.1. Exemption from tax; property of widowers

Section 2.1. There shall be further exempt from taxation the property of each widower, resident of this state, in the amount of:

1. One thousand five hundred dollars if the total assessment of such widower does not exceed three thousand five hundred dollars.

2. One thousand dollars if the total assessment of such widower does not exceed four thousand dollars.

3. Five hundred dollars if the total assessment of such widower does not exceed four thousand five hundred dollars.

4. Two hundred fifty dollars if the total assessment of such widower does not exceed five thousand dollars.

5. No exemption if the total assessment of such widower exceeds five thousand dollars.

In order to qualify for this exemption, the income from all sources of such widower, together with the income from all sources of all children of such widower residing with the widower in his residence in the year immediately preceding the year for which such widower applies for this exemption, shall not exceed:

1. Seven thousand dollars if none of the widower's children under the age of eighteen years resided with him in such widower's residence; or

2. Ten thousand dollars if one or more of the widower's children residing with him in such widower's residence was under the age of eighteen years, or was totally and permanently disabled, physically or mentally, as certified by competent medical authority as provided by law.

Such widower shall have resided with his last spouse in this state at the time of the spouse's death if he was not a widower and a resident of this state prior to January 1, 1969.

No property shall be exempt which has been conveyed to evade taxation. The total exemption from taxation granted to the property owned by a person who qualifies for any exemption in accordance with the terms of this section shall not exceed one thousand five hundred dollars. This section shall be self-executing.

2.2. Exemption from tax; property of persons who are disabled

Section 2.2. A. There shall be further exempt from taxation the property of each person who, after age seventeen, has been medically certified as totally and permanently disabled, in the amount of:

1. One thousand five hundred dollars if the total assessment of such person does not exceed three thousand five hundred dollars.

2. One thousand dollars if the total assessment of such person does not exceed four thousand dollars.

3. Five hundred dollars if the total assessment of such person does not exceed four thousand five hundred dollars.

4. Two hundred fifty dollars if the total assessment of such person does not exceed five thousand dollars.

5. No exemption if the total assessment of such person exceeds five thousand dollars. The legislature may by law prescribe criteria for medical certification of such disability.

B. The income from all sources of the person who is disabled, the person's spouse and all of the person's children who reside in the person's residence in the year immediately preceding the year for which the person applies for this exemption shall not exceed:

1. Seven thousand dollars if none of the person's children under the age of eighteen years resided in the person's residence; or

2. Ten thousand dollars if one or more of the person's children residing in the residence was under the age of eighteen years or was totally and permanently disabled, physically or mentally, as certified by competent medical authority as provided by law.

C. No property shall be exempt which has been conveyed to evade taxation. The total exemption from taxation granted to the property owned by a person who qualifies for any exemption in accordance with the terms of this section shall not exceed one thousand five hundred dollars. This section shall be self-executing.

2.3. Exemption from tax; increase in amount of exemptions, assessments and income

Section 2.3. The legislature may by law increase the amount of the exemptions, the total permissible amount of assessments or the permissible amount of income from all sources prescribed in sections 2, 2.1 and 2.2 of this article.

3. Annual tax; purposes; amount; tax laws; payment of taxes into state treasury

Section 3. The legislature shall provide by law for an annual tax sufficient, with other sources of revenue, to defray the necessary ordinary expenses of the state for each fiscal year. And for the purpose of paying the state debt, if there be any, the legislature shall provide for levying an annual tax sufficient to pay the annual interest and the principal of such debt within twenty-five years from the final passage of the law creating the debt.

No tax shall be levied except in pursuance of law, and every law imposing a tax shall state distinctly the object of the tax, to which object only it shall be applied.

All taxes levied and collected for state purposes shall be paid into the state treasury in money only.

4. Fiscal year; annual statement of receipts and expenditures; deficit

Section 4. The fiscal year shall commence on the first day of July in each year. An accurate statement of the receipts and expenditures of the public money shall be published annually, in such manner as shall be provided by law. Whenever the expenses of any fiscal year shall exceed the income, the legislature may provide for levying a tax for the ensuing fiscal year sufficient, with other sources of income, to pay the deficiency, as well as the estimated expenses of the ensuing fiscal year.

5. Power of state to contract debts; purposes; limit; restrictions

Section 5. The state may contract debts to supply the casual deficits or failures in revenues, or to meet expenses not otherwise provided for; but the aggregate amount of such debts, direct and contingent, whether contracted by virtue of one or more laws, or at different periods of time, shall never exceed the sum of three hundred and fifty thousand dollars; and the money arising from the creation of such debts shall be applied to the purpose for which it was obtained or to repay the debts so contracted, and to no other purpose.

In addition to the above limited power to contract debts the state may borrow money to repel invasion, suppress insurrection, or defend the state in time of war; but the money thus raised shall be applied exclusively to the object for which the loan shall have been authorized or to the repayment of the debt thereby created. No money shall be paid out of the state treasury, except in the manner provided by law.

6. Local assessments and taxes

Section 6. Incorporated cities, towns, and villages may be vested by law with power to make local improvements by special assessments, or by special taxation of property benefited. For all corporate purposes, all municipal corporations may be vested with authority to assess and collect taxes.

7. Gift or loan of credit; subsidies; stock ownership; joint ownership

Section 7. Neither the state, nor any county, city, town, municipality, or other subdivision of the state shall ever give or loan its credit in the aid of, or make any donation or grant, by subsidy or otherwise, to any individual, association, or corporation, or become a subscriber to, or a shareholder in, any company or corporation, or become a joint owner with any person, company, or corporation, except as to such ownerships as may accrue to the state by operation or provision of law or as authorized by law solely for investment of the monies in the various funds of the state.

8. Local debt limits; assent of taxpayers

Section 8. (1) No county, city, town, school district, or other municipal corporation shall for any purpose become indebted in any manner to an amount exceeding six per centum of the taxable property in such county, city, town, school district, or other municipal corporation, without the assent of a majority of the property taxpayers, who must also in all respects be qualified electors, therein voting at an election provided by law to be held for that purpose, the value of the taxable property therein to be ascertained by the last assessment for state and county purposes, previous to incurring such indebtedness; except, that in incorporated cities and towns assessments shall be taken from the last assessment for city or town purposes; provided, that under no circumstances shall any county or school district become indebted to an amount exceeding fifteen per centum of such taxable property, as shown by the last assessment roll thereof; and provided further, that any incorporated city or town, with such assent, may be allowed to become indebted to a larger amount, but not exceeding twenty per centum additional, for supplying such city or town with water, artificial light, or sewers, when the works for supplying such water, light, or sewers are or shall be owned and controlled by the municipality, and for the acquisition and development by the incorporated city or town of land or interests therein for open space preserves, parks, playgrounds and recreational facilities.

(2) The provisions of section 18, subsections (3), (4), (5) and (6) of this article shall not apply to this section.

8.1. Unified school district debt limit

Section 8.1. (1) Notwithstanding the provisions of section 8 of this article a unified school district may become indebted to an amount not exceeding thirty per cent of the taxable property of the school district, as shown by the last assessment roll thereof. For purposes of this section, a unified school district is a single school district which provides education to the area within the district for grades kindergarten through twelve and which area is not subject to taxation by any other common or high school district.

(2) The provisions of section 18, subsections (3), (4), (5) and (6) of this article shall not apply to this section.

9. Statement of tax and objects

Section 9. Every law which imposes, continues, or revives a tax shall distinctly state the tax and the objects for which it shall be applied; and it shall not be sufficient to refer to any other law to fix such tax or object.

10. Aid of church, private or sectarian school, or public service corporation

Section 10. No tax shall be laid or appropriation of public money made in aid of any church, or private or sectarian school, or any public service corporation.

11. Taxing procedure; license tax on registered vehicles

Section 11. From and after December 31, 1973, the manner, method and mode of assessing, equalizing and levying taxes in the state of Arizona shall be such as is prescribed by law.

From and after December 31, 1973, a license tax is hereby imposed on vehicles registered for operation upon the highways in Arizona, which license tax shall be in lieu of all ad valorem property taxes on any vehicle subject to such license tax. Such license tax shall be collected as provided by law. To facilitate an even distribution of the registration of vehicles and the collection of the license tax imposed by this section, the legislature may provide for different times or periods of registration between and within the several classes of vehicles.

In the event that a vehicle is destroyed after the beginning of a registration year, the license tax paid for such year on such vehicle may be reduced as provided by law.

From and after December 31, 1973, mobile homes, as defined by law for tax purposes, shall not be subject to the license tax imposed under the provisions of this section but shall be subject to ad valorem property taxes on any mobile homes in the manner provided by law. Distribution of the proceeds derived from such tax shall be as provided by law.

From and after December 31, 1973, the legislature shall provide for the distribution of the proceeds from such license tax to the state, counties, school districts, cities and towns.

12. Authority to provide for levy and collection of license and other taxes

Section 12. The law-making power shall have authority to provide for the levy and collection of license, franchise, gross revenue, excise, income, collateral and direct inheritance, legacy, and succession taxes, also graduated income taxes, graduated collateral and direct inheritance taxes, graduated legacy and succession taxes, stamp, registration, production, or other specific taxes.

13. Inventory, materials and products of manufacturers; production livestock and animals; tax exemption

Section 13. No tax shall be levied on:

1. Raw or unfinished materials, unassembled parts, work in process or finished products, constituting the inventory of a manufacturer or manufacturing establishment located within the state and principally engaged in the fabrication, production and manufacture of products, wares and articles for use, from raw or prepared materials, imparting thereto new forms, qualities, properties and combinations, which materials, parts, work in process or finished products are not consigned or billed to any other party.

2. Livestock, poultry, aquatic animals and honeybees owned by a person who is principally engaged in agricultural production, subject to such conditions as may be prescribed by law.

14. Use and distribution of vehicle, user, and gasoline and diesel tax receipts

Section 14. No moneys derived from fees, excises, or license taxes relating to registration, operation, or use of vehicles on the public highways or streets or to fuels or any other energy source used for the propulsion of vehicles on the public highways or streets, shall be expended for other than highway and street purposes including the cost of administering the state highway system and the laws creating such fees, excises, or license taxes, statutory refunds and adjustments provided by law, payment of principal and interest on highway and street bonds and obligations, expenses of state enforcement of traffic laws and state administration of traffic safety programs, payment of costs of publication and distribution of Arizona highways magazine, state costs of construction, reconstruction, maintenance or repair of public highways, streets or bridges, costs of rights of way acquisitions and expenses related thereto, roadside development, and for distribution to counties, incorporated cities and towns to be used by them solely for highway and street purposes including costs of rights of way acquisitions and expenses related thereto, construction, reconstruction, maintenance, repair, roadside development, of county, city and town roads, streets, and bridges and payment of principal and interest on highway and street bonds. As long as the total highway user revenues derived equals or exceeds the total derived in the fiscal year ending June 30, 1970, the state and any county shall not receive from such revenues for the use of each and for distribution to cities and towns, fewer dollars than were received and distributed in such fiscal year. This section shall not apply to moneys derived from the automobile license tax imposed under section 11 of article IX of the Constitution of Arizona. All moneys collected in accordance with this section shall be distributed as provided by law.

15. License tax on aircraft

Section 15. Commencing January 1, 1965, a license tax is imposed on aircraft registered for operation in Arizona, which license tax shall be in lieu of all ad valorem property taxes on any aircraft subject thereto, but nothing in this section shall be deemed to apply to:

1. Regularly scheduled aircraft operated by an air line company for the primary purpose of carrying persons or property for hire in interstate, intrastate, or international transportation.

2. Aircraft owned and held by an aircraft dealer solely for purposes of sale.

3. Aircraft owned by a nonresident who operates aircraft for a period not in excess of ninety days in any one calendar year, provided that such aircraft are not engaged in any intrastate commercial activity.

4. Aircraft owned and operated exclusively in the public service by the state or by any political subdivision thereof, or by the civil air patrol. The amount, manner, method and mode of assessing, equalizing and levying such license tax and the distribution of the proceeds therefrom shall be prescribed by law.

16. Exemption of watercraft from ad valorem property taxes

Section 16. Commencing January 1, 1967, all watercraft registered for operation in Arizona, excluding watercraft owned and operated for any commercial purpose, is exempt from ad valorem property taxes. Watercraft exempt from ad valorem property taxes shall be subject to or exempt from a license tax, as may be prescribed by law.

"Watercraft", as used in this section, shall be defined as provided by law.

17. Economic estimates commission; appropriation limitation; powers and duties of commission

Section 17. (1) The economic estimates commission shall be established by law, with a membership of not to exceed three members, and shall determine and publish prior to February 1 of each year the estimated total personal income for the following fiscal year. By April 1 of each year the commission shall determine and publish a final estimate of the total personal income for the following fiscal year, which estimate shall be used in computing the appropriations limit for the legislature. For the purposes of this section, "total personal income" means the dollar amount that will be reported as total income by persons for the state of Arizona by the U. S. department of commerce or its successor agency.

(2) For purposes of this section, "state revenues":

(a) Include all monies, revenues, fees, fines, penalties, funds, tuitions, property and receipts of any kind whatsoever received by or for the account of the state or any of its agencies, departments, offices, boards, commissions, authorities, councils and institutions except as provided in this subsection.

(b) Do not include:

(i) Any amounts or property received from the issuance or incurrence of bonds or other lawful long-term obligations issued or incurred for a specific purpose. For the purpose of this subdivision long-term obligations shall not include warrants issued in the ordinary course of operation or registered for payment by the state.

(ii) Any amounts or property received as payment of dividends or interest.

(iii) Any amounts or property received by the state in the capacity of trustee, custodian or agent.

(iv) Any amounts received from employers for deposit in the unemployment compensation fund or any successor fund.

(v) Any amounts collected by the state for distribution to counties, cities and towns without specific restrictions on the use of the funds other than the restrictions included in section 14 of this article.

(vi) Any amounts received as grants, aid, contributions or gifts of any type, except voluntary contributions or other contributions received directly or indirectly in lieu of taxes.

(vii) Any amounts received as the proceeds from the sale, lease or redemption of property or as consideration for services or the use of property.

(viii) Any amounts received pursuant to a transfer during a fiscal year from another agency, department, office, board, commission, authority, council or institution of the state which were included as state revenues for such fiscal year or which are excluded from state revenue under other provisions of this subsection.

(ix) Any amounts attributable to an increase in the rates of tax subsequent to July 1, 1979 on vehicle users, gasoline and diesel fuel which were levied on July 1, 1979.

(x) Any amounts received during a fiscal year as refunds, reimbursements or other recoveries of amounts appropriated which were applied against the appropriation limitation for such fiscal year or which were excluded from state revenues under other provisions of this subsection.

(3) The legislature shall not appropriate for any fiscal year state revenues in excess of seven per cent of the total personal income of the state for that fiscal year as determined by the economic estimates commission. The limitation may be exceeded upon affirmative vote of two-thirds of the membership of each house of the legislature on each measure that appropriates amounts in excess of the limitation. If the legislature authorizes a specific dollar amount of appropriation for more than one fiscal year, for the purpose of measuring such appropriation against the appropriation limitation, the entire amount appropriated shall be applied against the limitation in the first fiscal year during which any expenditures are authorized, and in no other fiscal year.

(4) In order to permit the transference of governmental functions or funding responsibilities between the federal and state governments and between the state government and its political subdivisions without abridging the purpose of this section to limit state appropriations to a percentage of total personal income, the legislature shall provide for adjustments of the appropriation percentage limitation consistent with the following principles:

(a) If the federal government assumes all or any part of the cost of providing a governmental function which the state previously funded in whole or in part, the appropriation limitation shall be commensurately decreased.

(b) If the federal government requires the state to assume all or any part of the cost of providing a governmental function the appropriation limitation shall be commensurately increased.

(c) If the state assumes all or any part of the cost of providing a governmental function and the state requires the political subdivision, which previously funded all or any part of the cost of the function to commensurately decrease its tax revenues, the appropriation percentage limitation shall be commensurately increased.

(d) If a political subdivision assumes all or any part of the cost of providing a governmental function previously funded in whole or in part by the state, the appropriation percentage limitation shall be commensurately decreased.

Any adjustments made pursuant to this subsection shall be made for the first fiscal year of the assumption of the cost. Such adjustment shall remain in effect for each subsequent fiscal year.

18. <u>Residential ad valorem tax limits; limit on increase in values; definitions</u>

Section 18. (1) The maximum amount of ad valorem taxes that may be collected from residential property in any tax year shall not exceed one per cent of the property's full cash value as limited by this section.

(2) The limitation provided in subsection (1) does not apply to:

(a) Ad valorem taxes or special assessments levied to pay the principal of and interest and redemption charges on bonded indebtedness or other lawful long-term obligations issued or incurred for a specific purpose.

(b) Ad valorem taxes or assessments levied by or for property improvement assessment districts, improvement districts and other special purpose districts other than counties, cities, towns, school districts and community college districts.

(c) Ad valorem taxes levied pursuant to an election to exceed a budget, expenditure or tax limitation.

(3) Except as otherwise provided by subsections (5), (6) and (7) of this section the value of real property and improvements and the value of mobile homes used for all ad valorem taxes except those specified in subsection (2) shall be the lesser of the full cash value of the property or an amount ten per cent greater than the value of property determined pursuant to this subsection for the prior year or an amount equal to the value of property determined pursuant to this subsection for the prior year plus one-fourth of the difference between such value and the full cash value of the property for current tax year, whichever is greater.

(4) The legislature shall by law provide a method of determining the value, subject to the provisions of subsection (3), of new property.

(5) The limitation on increases in the value of property prescribed in subsection (3) does not apply to equalization orders that the legislature specifically exempts by law from such limitation.

(6) Subsection (3) does not apply to:

(a) Property used in the business of patented or unpatented producing mines and the mills and the smelters operated in connection with the mines.

(b) Producing oil, gas and geothermal interests.

(c) Real property, improvements thereto and personal property used thereon used in the operation of telephone, telegraph, gas, water and electric utility companies.

(d) Aircraft that is regularly scheduled and operated by an airline company for the primary purpose of carrying persons or property for hire in interstate, intrastate or international transportation.

(e) Standing timber.

(f) Property used in the operation of pipelines.

(g) Personal property regardless of use except mobile homes.

(7) A resident of this state who is sixty-five years of age or older may apply to the county assessor for a property valuation protection option on the person's primary residence, including not more than ten acres of undeveloped appurtenant land. To be eligible for the property valuation protection option, the resident shall make application and furnish documentation required by the assessor on or before September 1. If the resident fails to file the application on or before September 1, the assessor shall process the application for the subsequent year. If the resident files an application with the assessor on or before September 1, the assessor shall notify the resident whether the application is accepted or denied on or before December 1. The resident may apply for a property valuation protection option after residing in the primary residence for two years. If one person owns the property, the person's total income from all sources including nontaxable income shall not exceed four hundred per cent of the supplemental security income benefit rate established by section 1611(b)(1) of the social security act. If the property is owned by two or more persons, including a husband and wife, at least one of the owners must be sixty-five years of age or older and the owners' combined total income from all sources including nontaxable income shall not exceed five hundred per cent of the supplemental security income benefit rate established by section 1611(b)(1) of the social security act. The assessor shall review the owner's income qualifications on a triennial basis and shall use the owner's average total income during the previous three years for the review. If the county assessor approves a property valuation protection option, the value of the primary residence shall remain fixed at the full cash value in effect during the year the property valuation protection option is filed and as long as the owner remains eligible. To remain eligible, the county assessor shall require a qualifying resident to reapply for the property valuation protection option every three years and shall send a notice of reapplication to qualifying residents six months before the three year reapplication requirement. If title to the property is conveyed to any person who does not qualify for the property valuation protection option, the property valuation protection option terminates, and the property shall revert to its current full cash value.

(8) The legislature shall provide by law a system of property taxation consistent with the provisions of this section.

(9) For purposes of this section:

(a) "Owner" means the owner of record of the property and includes a person who owns the majority beneficial interest of a living trust.

(b) "Primary residence" means all owner occupied real property and improvements to that real property in this state that is a single family home, condominium, townhouse or an 19.

Limitation on ad valorem tax levied; exceptions

Section 19. (1) The maximum amount of ad valorem taxes levied by any county, city, town or community college district shall not exceed an amount two per cent greater than the amount levied in the preceding year.

(2) The limitation prescribed by subsection (1) does not apply to:

(a) Ad valorem taxes or special assessments levied to pay the principal of and the interest and redemption charges on bonded indebtedness or other lawful long-term obligations issued or incurred for a specific purpose.

(b) Ad valorem taxes or assessments levied by or for property improvement assessment districts, improvement districts and other special purpose districts other than counties, cities, towns and community college districts.

(c) Ad valorem taxes levied by counties for support of common, high and unified school districts.

(3) This section applies to all tax years beginning after December 31, 1981.

(4) The limitation prescribed by subsection (1) shall be increased each year to the maximum permissible limit, whether or not the political subdivision actually levies ad valorem taxes to such amounts.

(5) The voters, in the manner prescribed by law, may elect to allow ad valorem taxation in excess of the limitation prescribed by this section.

(6) The limitation prescribed by subsection (1) of this section shall be increased by the amount of ad valorem taxes levied against property not subject to taxation in the prior year and shall be decreased by the amount of ad valorem taxes levied against property subject to taxation in the prior year and not subject to taxation in the current year. Such amounts of ad valorem taxes shall be computed using the rate applied to property not subject to this subsection.

(7) The legislature shall provide by law for the implementation of this section.

20. Expenditure limitation; adjustments; reporting

Section 20. (1) The economic estimates commission shall determine and publish prior to April 1 of each year the expenditure limitation for the following fiscal year for each county, city and town. The expenditure limitations shall be determined by adjusting the amount of actual payments of local revenues for each such political subdivision for fiscal year 1979-1980 to reflect the changes in the population of each political subdivision and the cost of living. The governing board of any political subdivision shall not authorize expenditures of local revenues in excess of the limitation prescribed in this section, except as provided in subsections (2), (6) and (9) of this section.

(2) Expenditures in excess of the limitations determined pursuant to subsection (1) of this section may be authorized as follows:

(a) Upon affirmative vote of two-thirds of the members of the governing board for expenditures directly necessitated by a natural or man-made disaster declared by the governor. Any expenditures in excess of the expenditure limitation, as authorized by this paragraph, shall not affect the determination of the expenditure limitation pursuant to subsection (1) of this section in any subsequent years. Any expenditures authorized pursuant to this paragraph shall be made either in the fiscal year in which the disaster is declared or in the succeeding fiscal year.

(b) Upon the affirmative vote of seventy per cent of the members of the governing board for expenditures directly necessitated by a natural or man-made disaster not declared by the governor, subject to the following:

(i) The governing board reducing expenditures below the expenditure limitation determined pursuant to subsection (1) of this section by the amount of the excess expenditure for the fiscal year following a fiscal year in which excess expenditures were made pursuant to this paragraph; or

(ii) Approval of the excess expenditure by a majority of the qualified electors voting either at a special election held by the governing board or at a regularly scheduled election for the nomination or election of the members of the governing board, in the manner provided by law. If the excess expenditure is not approved by a majority of the qualified electors voting, the governing board shall for the fiscal year which immediately follows the fiscal year in which the excess expenditures are made, reduce expenditures below the expenditure limitation determined pursuant to subsection (1) of this section by the amount of the excess expenditures. Any expenditures in excess of the expenditure limitation, as authorized by this paragraph, shall not affect the determination of the expenditure limitation pursuant to subsection (1) of this section in any subsequent years. Any expenditures pursuant to this paragraph shall be made either in the fiscal year in which the disaster occurs or in the succeeding fiscal year.

(c) Upon affirmative vote of at least two-thirds of the members of the governing board and approval by a majority of the qualified electors voting either at a special election held by the governing board in a manner prescribed by law, or at a regularly scheduled election for the nomination or election of the members of the governing board. Such approval by a majority of the qualified electors voting shall be for a specific amount in excess of the expenditure limitation, and such approval must occur prior to the fiscal year in which the expenditure limitation is to be exceeded. Any expenditures in excess of the expenditure limitation, as authorized by this subdivision, shall not affect the determination of the expenditure limitation pursuant to subsection (1) of this section, in subsequent years.

(3) As used in this section:

(a) "Base limit" means the amount of actual payments of local revenues for fiscal year 1979-1980 as used to determine the expenditure limitation pursuant to subsection (1) of this section.

(b) "Cost of living" means either:

(i)   The price of goods and services as measured by the implicit price deflator for the gross national product or its successor as reported by the United States department of commerce or its successor agency.

(ii) A different measure or index of the cost of living adopted at the direction of the legislature, by concurrent resolution, upon affirmative vote of two-thirds of the membership of each house of the legislature. Such measure or index shall apply for subsequent fiscal years, except it shall not apply for the fiscal year following the adoption of such measure or index if the measure or index is adopted after March 1 of the preceding fiscal year.

(c) "Expenditure" means any authorization for the payment of local revenues.

(d) "Local revenues" includes all monies, revenues, funds, fees, fines, penalties, tuitions, property and receipts of any kind whatsoever received by or for the account of a political subdivision or any of its agencies, departments, offices, boards, commissions, authorities, councils and institutions, except:

(i)   Any amounts or property received from the issuance or incurrence of bonds or other lawful long-term obligations issued or incurred for a specific purpose, or collected or segregated to make payments or deposits required by a contract concerning such bonds or obligations. For the purpose of this subdivision long-term obligations shall not include warrants issued in the ordinary course of operation or registered for payment, by a political subdivision.

(ii) Any amounts or property received as payment of dividends or interest, or any gain on the sale or redemption of investment securities, the purchase of which is authorized by law.

(iii) Any amounts or property received by a political subdivision in the capacity of trustee, custodian or agent.

(iv) Any amounts received as grants and aid of any type received from the federal government or any of its agencies.

(v) Any amounts received as grants, aid, contributions or gifts of any type except amounts received directly or indirectly in lieu of taxes received directly or indirectly from any private agency or organization or any individual.

(vi) Any amounts received from the state which are included within the appropriation limitation prescribed in section 17 of this article.

(vii) Any amounts received pursuant to a transfer during a fiscal year from another agency, department, office, board, commission, authority, council or institution of the same political subdivision which were included as local revenues for such fiscal year or which are excluded from local revenue under other provisions of this section.

(viii) Any amounts or property accumulated for the purpose of purchasing land, buildings or improvements or constructing buildings or improvements, if such accumulation and purpose have been approved by the voters of the political subdivision.

(ix) Any amounts received pursuant to section 14 of this article which are greater than the amount received in fiscal year 1979-1980.

(x) Any amounts received in return for goods or services pursuant to a contract with another political subdivision, school district, community college district or the state, and expended by the other political subdivision, school district, community college district or the state pursuant to the expenditure limitation in effect when the amounts are expended by the other political subdivision, school district, community college district or the state.

(xi) Any amounts expended for the construction, reconstruction, operation or maintenance of a hospital financially supported by a city or town prior to January 1, 1980.

(xii) Any amounts or property collected to pay the principal of and interest on any warrants issued by a political subdivision and outstanding as of July 1, 1979.

(xiii) Any amounts received during a fiscal year as refunds, reimbursements or other recoveries of amounts expended which were applied against the expenditure limitation for such fiscal year or which were excluded from local revenues under other provisions of this subsection.

(xiv) Any amounts received collected by the counties for distribution to school districts pursuant to state law.

(e) "Political subdivision" means any county, city or town. This definition applies only to this section and does not otherwise modify the commonly accepted definition of political subdivision.

(f) "Population" means either:

(i) The periodic census conducted by the United States department of commerce or its successor agency, or the annual update of such census by the department of economic security or its successor agency.

(ii) A different measure or index of population adopted at the direction of the legislature, by concurrent resolution, upon affirmative vote of two-thirds of the membership of each house of the legislature. Such measure or index shall apply for subsequent fiscal years, except it shall not apply for the fiscal year following the adoption of such measure or index if the measure or index is adopted after March 1 of the preceding fiscal year.

(4) The economic estimates commission shall adjust the base limit to reflect subsequent transfers of all or any part of the cost of providing a governmental function, in a manner prescribed by law. The adjustment provided for in this subsection shall be used in determining the expenditure limitation pursuant to subsection (1) of this section beginning with the fiscal year immediately following the transfer.

(5) The economic estimates commission shall adjust the base limit to reflect any subsequent annexation, creation of a new political subdivision, consolidation or change in the boundaries of a political subdivision, in a manner prescribed by law. The adjustment provided for in this subsection shall be used in determining the expenditure limitation pursuant to subsection (1) of this section beginning with the fiscal year immediately following the annexation, creation of a new political subdivision, consolidation or change in the boundaries of a political subdivision.

(6) Any political subdivision may adjust the base limit by the affirmative vote of two-thirds of the members of the governing board or by initiative, in the manner provided by law, and in either instance by approval of the proposed adjustment by a majority of the qualified electors voting at a regularly scheduled general election or at a nonpartisan election held for the nomination or election of the members of the governing board. The impact of the modification of the expenditure limitation shall appear on the ballot and in publicity pamphlets, as provided by law. Any adjustment, pursuant to this subsection, of the base limit shall be used in determining the expenditure limitation pursuant to subsection (1) of this section beginning with the fiscal year immediately following the approval, as provided by law.

(7) The legislature shall provide for expenditure limitations for such special districts as it deems necessary.

(8) The legislature shall establish by law a uniform reporting system for all political subdivisions or special districts subject to an expenditure limitation pursuant to this section to insure compliance with this section. The legislature shall establish by law sanctions and penalties for failure to comply with this section.

(9) Subsection (1) of this section does not apply to a city or town which at a regularly scheduled election for the nomination or election of members of the governing board of the city or town adopts an expenditure limitation pursuant to this subsection different from the expenditure limitation prescribed by subsection (1) of this section. The governing board of a city or town may by a two-thirds vote provide for referral of an alternative expenditure limitation or the qualified electors may by initiative, in the manner provided by law, propose an alternative expenditure limitation. In a manner provided by law, the impact of the alternative expenditure limitation shall be compared to the impact of the expenditure limitation prescribed by subsection (1) of this section, and the comparison shall appear on the ballot and in publicity pamphlets. If a majority of the qualified electors voting on such issue vote in favor of the alternative expenditure limitation, such limitation shall apply to the city or town. If more than one alternative expenditure limitation is on the ballot and more than one alternative expenditure limitation is approved by the voters, the alternative expenditure limitation receiving the highest number of votes shall apply to such city or town. If an alternative expenditure limitation is adopted, it shall apply for the four succeeding fiscal years. Following the fourth succeeding fiscal year, the expenditure limitation prescribed by subsection (1) of this section shall become the expenditure limitation for the city or town unless an alternative expenditure limitation is approved as provided in this subsection. If a majority of the qualified electors voting on such issue vote against an alternative expenditure limitation, the expenditure limitation prescribed pursuant to subsection (1) of this section shall apply to the city or town, and no new alternative expenditure limitation may be submitted to the voters for a period of at least two years. If an alternative expenditure limitation is adopted pursuant to this subsection, the city or town may not conduct an override election provided for in section 19, subsection (4) of this article, during the time period in which the alternative expenditure limitation is in effect.

(10) This section does not apply to any political subdivision until the fiscal year immediately following the first regularly scheduled election after July 1, 1980 for the nomination or election of the members of the governing board of such political subdivision, except that a political subdivision, prior to the fiscal year during which the spending limitation would first become effective, may modify the expenditure limitation prescribed pursuant to subsection (1) of this section, by the provisions prescribed by subsections (2) and (6) of this section, or may adopt an alternative expenditure limitation pursuant to subsection (9) of this section.

A county may conduct a special election to exceed the expenditure limitation prescribed pursuant to subsection (1) of this section for the fiscal years 1982-1983 and 1983-1984, on the first Tuesday after the first Monday in November in 1981.

(11) City", as used in this article, means city or charter city.

21. <u>Expenditure limitations for school districts and community college districts</u>

Section 21. (1) The economic estimates commission shall determine and publish prior to April 1 of each year the expenditure limitation for the following fiscal year for each community college district. The expenditure limitations shall be determined by adjusting the amount of expenditures of local revenues for each such district for fiscal year 1979-1980 to reflect the changes in the student population of each district and the cost of living. The governing board of any community college district shall not authorize expenditures of local revenues in excess of the limitation prescribed in this section, except in the manner provided by law.

(2) The economic estimates commission shall determine and publish prior to May 1 of each year the aggregate expenditure limitation for all school districts for the following fiscal year. The aggregate expenditure limitation shall be determined by adjusting the total amount of expenditures of local revenues for all school districts for fiscal year 1979-1980 to reflect the changes in student population in the school districts and the cost of living, and multiplying the result by 1.10. The aggregate expenditures of local revenues for all school districts shall not exceed the limitation prescribed in this section, except as provided in subsection (3) of this section.

(3) Expenditures in excess of the limitation determined pursuant to subsection (2) of this section may be authorized by the legislature for a single fiscal year, by concurrent resolution, upon affirmative vote of two-thirds of the membership of each house of the legislature.

(4) As used in this section:

(a) "Cost of living" means either:

(i) The price of goods and services as measured by the implicit price deflator for the gross national product or its successor as reported by the United States department of commerce, or its successor agency.

(ii) A different measure or index of the cost of living adopted at the direction of the legislature, by concurrent resolution, upon affirmative vote of two-thirds of the membership of each house of the legislature. Such measure or index shall apply for subsequent fiscal years, except it shall not apply for the fiscal year following the adoption of such measure or index if the measure or index is adopted after March 1 of the preceding fiscal year.

(b) "Expenditure" means any amounts budgeted to be paid from local revenues as prescribed by law.

(c) "Local revenues" includes all monies, revenues, funds, property and receipts of any kind whatsoever received by or for the account of a school district or community college district or any of its agencies, departments, offices, boards, commissions, authorities, councils and institutions, except:

(i) Any amounts or property received from the issuance or incurrence of bonds, or other lawful long-term obligations issued or incurred for a specific purpose, or any amounts or property collected or segregated to make payments or deposits required by a contract concerning such bonds or obligations. For the purpose of this subdivision long-term obligations shall not include warrants issued in the ordinary course of operation or registered for payment by a political subdivision.

(ii) Any amounts or property received as payment of dividends and interest, or any gain on the sale or redemption of investment securities, the purchase of which is authorized by law.

(iii) Any amounts or property received by a school district or community college district in the capacity of trustee, custodian or agent.

(iv) Any amounts received as grants and aid of any type received from the federal government or any of its agencies except school assistance in federally affected areas.

(v) Any amounts or property received as grants, gifts, aid or contributions of any type except amounts received directly or indirectly in lieu of taxes received directly or indirectly from any private agency or organization, or any individual.

(vi) Any amounts received from the state for the purpose of purchasing land, buildings or improvements or constructing buildings or improvements.

(vii) Any amounts received pursuant to a transfer during a fiscal year from another agency, department, office, board, commission, authority, council or institution of the same community college district or school district which were included as local revenues for such fiscal year or which are excluded from local revenue under other provisions of this subsection.

(viii) Any amounts or property accumulated by a community college district for the purpose of purchasing land, buildings or improvements or constructing buildings or improvements.

(ix) Any amounts received in return for goods or services pursuant to a contract with another political subdivision, school district, community college district or the state and expended by the other political subdivision, school district, community college district or the state pursuant to the expenditure limitation in effect when the amounts are expended by the other political subdivision, school district, community college district or the state.

(x) Any amounts received as tuition or fees directly or indirectly from any public or private agency or organization or any individual.

(xi) Any ad valorem taxes received pursuant to an election to exceed the limitation prescribed by section 19 of this article or for the purposes of funding expenditures in excess of the expenditure limitations prescribed by subsection (7) of this section.

(xii) Any amounts received during a fiscal year as refunds, reimbursements or other recoveries of amounts expended which were applied against the expenditure limitation for such fiscal year or which were excluded from local revenues under other provisions of this subsection.

(d) For the purpose of subsection (2) of this section, the following items are also excluded from local revenues of school districts:

(i) Any amounts received as the proceeds from the sale, lease or rental of school property as authorized by law.

(ii) Any amounts received from the capital levy as authorized by law.

(iii) Any amounts received from the acquisition, operation, or maintenance of school services of a commercial nature which are entirely or predominantly self-supporting.

(iv) Any amounts received for the purpose of funding expenditures authorized in the event of destruction of or damage to the facilities of a school district as authorized by law.

(v) Any revenues derived from an additional state transaction privilege tax rate increment for educational purposes that was authorized by the voters before January 1, 2001.

(vi) Any amounts received pursuant to article XI, section 8, Constitution of Arizona, that are approved by the majority of qualified voters at a statewide general election held after November 1, 2002, and before January 1, 2003.

(e) "Student population" means the number of actual, full-time or the equivalent of actual full-time students enrolled in the school district or community college district determined in a manner prescribed by law.

(5) The economic estimates commission shall adjust the amount of expenditures of local revenues in fiscal year 1979-1980, as used to determine the expenditure limitation pursuant to subsection (1) or (2) of this section, to reflect subsequent transfers of all or any part of the cost of providing a governmental function, in a manner prescribed by law. The adjustment provided for in this subsection shall be used in determining the expenditure limitation pursuant to subsection (1) or (2) of this section beginning with the fiscal year immediately following the transfer.

(6) The economic estimates commission shall adjust the amount of expenditures of local revenues in fiscal year 1979-1980, as used to determine the expenditure limitation of a community college district pursuant to subsection (1) of this section, to reflect any subsequent annexation, creation of a new district, consolidation or change in the boundaries of a district, in a manner prescribed by law. The adjustment provided for in this subsection shall be used in determining the expenditure limitation pursuant to subsection (1) of this section beginning with the fiscal year immediately following the annexation, creation of a new district, consolidation or change in the boundaries of a district.

(7) The legislature shall establish by law expenditure limitations for each school district beginning with the fiscal year beginning July 1, 1980. Expenditures by a school district in excess of such an expenditure limitation must be approved by a majority of the electors voting on the excess expenditures.

(8) The legislature shall establish by law a uniform reporting system for school districts and community college districts to ensure compliance with this section. The legislature shall establish by law sanctions and penalties for failure to comply with this section.

22. Vote required to increase state revenues; application; exceptions

(A) An act that provides for a net increase in state revenues, as described in subsection B is effective on the affirmative vote of two-thirds of the members of each house of the legislature. If the act receives such an affirmative vote, it becomes effective immediately on the signature of the governor as provided by article IV, part 1, section 1. If the governor vetoes the measure, it shall not become effective unless it is approved by an affirmative vote of three-fourths of the members of each house of the legislature.

(B) The requirements of this section apply to any act that provides for a net increase in state revenues in the form of:

1. The imposition of any new tax.

2. An increase in a tax rate or rates.

3. A reduction or elimination of a tax deduction, exemption, exclusion, credit or other tax exemption feature in computing tax liability.

4. An increase in a statutorily prescribed state fee or assessment or an increase in a statutorily prescribed maximum limit for an administratively set fee.

5. The imposition of any new state fee or assessment or the authorization of any new administratively set fee.

6. The elimination of an exemption from a statutorily prescribed state fee or assessment.

7. A change in the allocation among the state, counties or cities of Arizona transaction privilege, severance, jet fuel and use, rental occupancy, or other taxes.

8. Any combination of the elements described in paragraphs 1 through 7.

(C) This section does not apply to:

1. The effects of inflation, increasing assessed valuation or any other similar effect that increases state revenue but is not caused by an affirmative act of the legislature.

2. Fees and assessments that are authorized by statute, but are not prescribed by formula, amount or limit, and are set by a state officer or agency.

3. Taxes, fees or assessments that are imposed by counties, cities, towns and other political subdivisions of this state.

(D) Each act to which this section applies shall include a separate provision describing the requirements for enactment prescribed by this section.

23. Expenditures required by initiative or referendum; funding source

Section 23. A. An initiative or referendum measure that proposes a mandatory expenditure of state revenues for any purpose, establishes a fund for any specific purpose or allocates funding for any specific purpose must also provide for an increased source of revenues sufficient to cover the entire immediate and future costs of the proposal. the increased revenues may not be derived from the state general fund or reduce or cause a reduction in general fund revenues.

B. If the identified revenue source provided pursuant to subsection a in any fiscal year fails to fund the entire mandated expenditure for that fiscal year, the legislature may reduce the expenditure of state revenues for that purpose in that fiscal year to the amount of funding supplied by the identified revenue source.

Article 10

STATE AND SCHOOL LANDS

1. Acceptance and holding of lands by state in trust

Section 1. All lands expressly transferred and confirmed to the state by the provisions of the Enabling Act approved June 20, 1910, including all lands granted to the state and all lands heretofore granted to the Territory of Arizona, and all lands otherwise acquired by the state, shall be by the state accepted and held in trust to be disposed of in whole or in part, only in manner as in the said Enabling Act and in this Constitution provided, and for the several objects specified in the respective granting and confirmatory provisions. The natural products and money proceeds of any of said lands shall be subject to the same trusts as the lands producing the same.

2. Unauthorized disposition of land or proceeds as breach of trust

Section 2. Disposition of any of said lands, or of any money or thing of value directly or indirectly derived therefrom, for any object other than that for which such particular lands (or the lands from which such money or thing of value shall have been derived) were granted or confirmed, or in any manner contrary to the provisions of the said Enabling Act, shall be deemed a breach of trust.

3. Mortgage or other encumbrance; sale or lease at public auction

Section 3. No mortgage or other encumbrance of the said lands, or any part thereof, shall be valid in favor of any person or for any purpose or under any circumstances whatsoever. Said lands shall not be sold or leased, in whole or in part, except to the highest and best bidder at a public auction to be held at the county seat of the county wherein the lands to be affected, or the major portion thereof, shall lie, notice of which public auction shall first have been duly given by advertisement, which shall set forth the nature, time and place of the transaction to be had, with a full description of the lands to be offered, and be published once each week for not less than ten successive weeks in a newspaper of general circulation published regularly at the state capital, and in that newspaper of like circulation which shall then be regularly published nearest to the location of the lands so offered; nor shall any sale or contract for the sale of any timber or other natural product of such lands be made, save at the place, in the manner, and after the notice by publication provided for sales and leases of the lands themselves. Nothing herein, or elsewhere in article X contained, shall prevent:

1. The leasing of any of the lands referred to in this article in such manner as the legislature may prescribe, for grazing, agricultural, commercial and homesite purposes, for a term of ten years or less, without advertisement;

2. The leasing of any of said lands, in such manner as the legislature may prescribe, whether or not also leased for grazing and agricultural purposes, for mineral purposes, other than for the exploration, development, and production of oil, gas and other hydrocarbon substances, for a term of twenty years or less, without advertisement, or,

3. The leasing of any of said lands, whether or not also leased for other purposes, for the exploration, development, and production of oil, gas and other hydrocarbon substances on, in or under said lands for an initial term of twenty (20) years or less and as long thereafter as oil, gas or other hydrocarbon substance may be procured therefrom in paying quantities, the leases to be made in any manner, with or without advertisement, bidding, or appraisement, and under such terms and provisions, as the legislature may prescribe, the terms and provisions to include a reservation of a royalty to the state of not less than twelve and one-half per cent of production.

4. Sale or other disposal; appraisal; minimum price; credit; passing of title

Section 4. All lands, lease-holds, timber, and other products of land, before being offered, shall be appraised at their true value, and no sale or other disposal thereof shall be made for a consideration less than the value so ascertained, nor in any case less than the minimum price hereinafter fixed, nor upon credit unless accompanied by ample security, and the legal title shall not be deemed to have passed until the consideration shall have been paid.

5. Minimum price; relinquishment of lands to United States

Section 5. No lands shall be sold for less than three dollars per acre, and no lands which are or shall be susceptible of irrigation under any projects now or hereafter completed or adopted by the United States under legislation for the reclamation of lands, or under any other project for the reclamation of lands, shall be sold at less than twenty-five dollars per acre; Provided, that the state, at the request of the secretary of the interior, shall from time to time relinquish such of its lands to the United States as at any time are needed for irrigation works in connection with any such government project, and other lands in lieu thereof shall be selected from lands of the character named and in the manner prescribed in section twenty-four of the said Enabling Act.

6. Lands reserved by United States for development of water power

Section 6. No lands reserved and excepted of the lands granted to this state by the United States, actually or prospectively valuable for the development of water powers or power for hydro-electric use or transmission, which shall be ascertained and designated by the secretary of the interior within five years after the proclamation of the president declaring the admission of the state, shall be subject to any disposition whatsoever by the state or by any officer of the state, and any conveyance or transfer of such lands made within said five years shall be null and void.

7. Establishment of permanent funds; segregation, investment and distribution of monies

Section 7. A. A separate permanent fund shall be established for each of the several objects for which the said grants are made and confirmed by the enabling act to the state, and whenever any monies shall be in any manner derived from any of said lands, the same shall be deposited by the state treasurer in the permanent fund corresponding to the grant under which the particular land producing such monies was, by the enabling act, conveyed or confirmed.

B. No monies shall ever be taken from one permanent fund for deposit in any other, or for any object other than that for which the land producing the same was granted or confirmed.

C. All such monies shall be invested in safe interest-bearing securities and prudent equity securities consistent with the requirements of this section.

D. The legislature shall establish a board of investment to serve as trustees of the permanent funds. The board shall provide for the management of the assets of the funds consistent with the following conditions:

1. Not more than sixty per cent of a fund at cost may be invested in equities at any time.

2. Equities that are eligible for purchase are restricted to stocks listed on any national stock exchange or eligible for trading through the United States national association of securities dealers automated quotation system, or successor institutions, except as may be prohibited by general criteria or by a restriction on investment in a specific security adopted pursuant to this subsection.

3. Not more than five per cent of all of the funds combined at cost may be invested in equity securities issued by the same institution, agency or corporation, other than securities issued as direct obligations of and fully guaranteed by the United States government.

E. In making investments under this section the state treasurer and trustees shall exercise the judgment and care under the prevailing circumstances that an institutional investor of ordinary prudence, discretion and intelligence exercises in managing large investments entrusted to it, not in regard to speculation, but in regard to the permanent disposition of monies, considering the probable safety of capital as well as the probable total rate of return over extended periods of time.

F. The earnings, interest, dividends and realized capital gains and losses from investment of a permanent fund, shall be credited to that fund.

G. The board of investment shall determine the amount of the annual distributions required by this section and allocate distributions pursuant to law. Beginning July 1, 2000 and except as otherwise provided in this section, the amount of the annual distribution from a permanent fund established pursuant to this section is the amount determined by multiplying the following factors:

1. The average of the annual total rate of return for the immediately preceding five complete fiscal years less the average of the annual percentage change in the GDP price deflator, or a successor index, for the immediately preceding five complete fiscal years. For purposes of this paragraph:

(a) "Annual total rate of return" means the quotient obtained by dividing the amount credited to a fund pursuant to subsection F for a complete fiscal year, plus unrealized capital gains and losses, by the average monthly market value of the fund for that year.

(b) "GDP price deflator" means the gross domestic price deflator reported by the United States department of commerce, bureau of economic analysis, or its successor agency.

2. The average of the monthly market values of the fund for the immediately preceding five complete fiscal years.

H. Notwithstanding any other provision of this section, the annual distribution from the permanent funds for fiscal years 1999-2000 through 2002-2003 shall be as follows:

1. For fiscal year 1999-2000, the greater of five per cent of the average of the monthly market values of the funds for fiscal years 1994-1995 through 1998-1999 or the average of actual annual distributions for fiscal years 1994-1995 through 1998-1999.

2. For fiscal years 2000-2001 through 2002-2003, the greater of the average of the actual annual distributions for the immediately preceding five complete fiscal years or the amount of the distribution required by subsection G.

8. Conformity of contracts with enabling act

Section 8. Every sale, lease, conveyance, or contract of or concerning any of the lands granted or confirmed, or the use thereof or the natural products thereof made to this state by the said Enabling Act, not made in substantial conformity with the provisions thereof, shall be null and void.

9. Sale or lease; conditions; limitations; lease prior to adoption of constitution

Section 9. All lands expressly transferred and confirmed to the state, by the provisions of the Enabling Act approved June 20, 1910, including all lands granted to the state, and all lands heretofore granted to the territory of Arizona, and all lands otherwise acquired by the state, may be sold or leased by the state in the manner, and on the conditions, and with the limitations, prescribed by the said Enabling Act and this Constitution, and as may be further prescribed by law; Provided, that the legislature shall provide for the separate appraisement of the lands and of the improvements on school and university lands which have been held under lease prior to the adoption of this Constitution, and for reimbursement to the actual bona fide residents or lessees of such lands upon which such improvements are situated, as prescribed by title 65, Civil Code of Arizona, 1901, and in such cases only as permit reimbursements to lessees in said title 65.

10. Laws for sale or lease of state lands; protection of residents and lessees

Section 10. The legislature shall provide by proper laws for the sale of all state lands or the lease of such lands, and shall further provide by said laws for the protection of the actual bona fide residents and lessees of said lands, whereby such residents and lessees of said lands shall be protected in their rights to their improvements (including water rights) in such manner that in case of lease to other parties the former lessee shall be paid by the succeeding lessee the value of such improvements and rights and actual bona fide residents and lessees shall have preference to a renewal of their leases at a reassessed rental to be fixed as provided by law.

11. Maximum acreage allowed single purchaser

Section 11. No individual, corporation or association shall be allowed to purchase more than one hundred sixty (160) acres of agricultural land or more than six hundred forty (640) acres of grazing land.

Article XI

EDUCATION

1. Public school system; education of pupils who are hearing and vision impaired

Section 1. A. The legislature shall enact such laws as shall provide for the establishment and maintenance of a general and uniform public school system, which system shall include:

1. Kindergarten schools.

2. Common schools.

3. High schools.

4. Normal schools.

5. Industrial schools.

6. Universities, which shall include an agricultural college, a school of mines, and such other technical schools as may be essential, until such time as it may be deemed advisable to establish separate state institutions of such character.

B. The legislature shall also enact such laws as shall provide for the education and care of pupils who are hearing and vision impaired.

2. Conduct and supervision of school system

Section 2. The general conduct and supervision of the public school system shall be vested in a state board of education, a state superintendent of public instruction, county school superintendents, and such governing boards for the state institutions as may be provided by law.

3. State board of education; composition; powers and duties; compensation

Section 3. The state board of education shall be composed of the following members: the superintendent of public instruction, the president of a state university or a state college, four lay members, a president or chancellor of a community college district, a person who is an owner or administrator of a charter school, a superintendent of a high school district, a classroom teacher and a county school superintendent. Each member, other than the superintendent of public instruction, shall be appointed by the governor with the consent of the senate in the manner prescribed by law. The powers, duties, compensation and expenses, and the terms of office, of the board shall be such as may be prescribed by law.

4. State superintendent of public instruction; board membership; powers and duties

Section 4. The state superintendent of public instruction shall be a member, and secretary, of the state board of education, and, ex-officio, a member of any other board having control of public instruction in any state institution. His powers and duties shall be prescribed by law.

5. Regents of university and other governing boards; appointments by governor; membership of governor on board of regents

Section 5. The regents of the university, and the governing boards of other state educational institutions, shall be appointed by the governor with the consent of the senate in the manner prescribed by law, except that the governor shall be, ex-officio, a member of the board of regents of the university.

6. Admission of students of both sexes to state educational institutions; tuition; common school system

Section 6. The university and all other state educational institutions shall be open to students of both sexes, and the instruction furnished shall be as nearly free as possible. The legislature shall provide for a system of common schools by which a free school shall be established and maintained in every school district for at least six months in each year, which school shall be open to all pupils between the ages of six and twenty-one years.

7. Sectarian instruction; religious or political test or qualification

Section 7. No sectarian instruction shall be imparted in any school or state educational institution that may be established under this Constitution, and no religious or political test or qualification shall ever be required as a condition of admission into any public educational institution of the state, as teacher, student, or pupil; but the liberty of conscience hereby secured shall not be so construed as to justify practices or conduct inconsistent with the good order, peace, morality, or safety of the state, or with the rights of others.

8. Permanent state school fund; source; apportionment of state funds

Section 8. A. A permanent state school fund for the use of the common schools shall be derived from the sale of public school lands or other public lands specified in the enabling act approved June 20, 1910; from all estates or distributive shares of estates that may escheat to the state; from all unclaimed shares and dividends of any corporation incorporated under the laws of Arizona; and from all gifts, devises, or bequests made to the state for general educational purposes.

B. The rental derived from school lands, with such other funds as may be provided by law shall be apportioned only for common and high school education in Arizona, and in such manner as may be prescribed by law.

9. County school fund; size of fund; free schools

Section 9. The amount of this apportionment shall become a part of the county school fund, and the legislature shall enact such laws as will provide for increasing the county fund sufficiently to maintain all the public schools of the county for a minimum term of six months in every school year. The laws of the state shall enable cities and towns to maintain free high schools, industrial schools, and commercial schools.

10. Source of revenue for maintenance of state educational institutions

Section 10. The revenue for the maintenance of the respective state educational institutions shall be derived from the investment of the proceeds of the sale, and from the rental of such lands as have been set aside by the enabling act approved June 20, 1910, or other legislative enactment of the United States, for the use and benefit of the respective state educational institutions. In addition to such income the legislature shall make such appropriations, to be met by taxation, as shall insure the proper maintenance of all state educational institutions, and shall make such special appropriations as shall provide for their development and improvement.

Article XII

COUNTIES

1. Counties as bodies politic and corporate

Section 1. Each county of the state, now or hereafter organized, shall be a body politic and corporate.

2. Counties of territory as counties of state

Section 2. The several counties of the territory of Arizona as fixed by statute at the time of the adoption of this Constitution are hereby declared to be the counties of the state until changed by law.

3. County officers; election; term of office

Section 3. There are hereby created in and for each organized county of the state the following officers who shall be elected by the qualified electors thereof: a sheriff, a county attorney, a recorder, a treasurer, an assessor, a superintendent of schools and at least three supervisors, each of whom shall be elected and hold his office for a term of four (4) years beginning on the first of January next after his election, which number of supervisors is subject to increase by law. The supervisors shall be nominated and elected from districts as provided by law.

The candidates for these offices elected in the general election of November 3, 1964 shall take office on the first day of January, 1965 and shall serve until the first day of January, 1969.

4. County officers; duties, powers, and qualifications; salaries

Section 4. The duties, powers, and qualifications of such officers shall be as prescribed by law. The board of supervisors of each county is hereby empowered to fix salaries for all county and precinct officers within such county for whom no compensation is provided by law, and the salaries so fixed shall remain in full force and effect until changed by general law.

5. Charter committee; charter preparation; approval

Section 5. A. The board of supervisors of any county with a population of more than five hundred thousand persons as determined by the most recent United States decennial or special census may call for an election to cause a charter committee to be elected by the qualified electors of that county at any time. Alternatively, the board of supervisors of any county with a population of more than five hundred thousand persons as determined by the most recent United States decennial or special census shall call for the election of the charter committee within ten days after receipt by the clerk of the board of supervisors of a petition that demands the election and that is signed by a number of qualified electors of the county at least equal to ten per cent of the total number of ballots cast for all candidates for governor or presidential electors in the county at the last preceding general election. The election shall be held at least one hundred days but not more than one hundred twenty days after the call for the election. Except as otherwise provided in this section, for elections held under this section or section 6 of this article, the manner of conducting and voting at an election, contesting an election, canvassing votes and certifying returns shall be the same, as nearly as practicable, as in elections for county officers.

B. At the election a vote shall be taken to elect members of the charter committee who will function if further proceedings are authorized and the ballot shall contain the question of whether further proceedings toward adopting a charter shall be authorized pursuant to the call for the election. Unless a majority of the qualified electors voting on the question votes to authorize further proceedings, the election of members of the charter committee shall be invalidated and no further proceedings may be had except pursuant to a subsequent call pursuant to subsection A.

C. The charter committee shall be composed of fifteen qualified electors of the county elected by supervisorial district with the same number serving from each district. A nomination petition for election to the charter committee shall be made available by the clerk of the board of supervisors and shall be signed by a number of qualified electors of the supervisorial district who are eligible to vote for the nominee at least equal to one per cent of the total number of ballots cast for all candidates for governor or presidential electors in the supervisorial district at the last preceding general election, and filed with the clerk not later than sixty days before the election. All qualified electors of the county, including all elected public officials, are eligible to seek election to the charter committee.

D. Within one hundred eighty days after the election the charter committee shall prepare and submit a proposed charter for the county. The proposed charter shall be signed by a majority of the members of the committee and filed with the clerk of the board of supervisors, after which the charter committee shall be dissolved. The county shall then publish the proposed charter in the official newspaper of the county at least once a week for three consecutive weeks. The first publication shall be made within twenty days after the proposed charter is filed with the clerk of the board of supervisors.

E. At least forty-five days but not more than sixty days after final publication, the proposed charter shall be submitted to the vote of the qualified electors of the county at a general or special election. If a general election will be held within ninety days after final publication, the charter shall be submitted at that general election. The full text of the proposed charter shall be printed in a publicity pamphlet and mailed to each household containing a registered voter at least eleven days before the charter election and the ballot may contain only a summary of the proposed charter provisions. The ballot shall contain a question regarding approval of the proposed charter and the questions pertaining to taxation authority and appointment of officers, if any, provided for in sections 7 and 8 of this article.

F. If a majority of the qualified electors voting ratifies the proposed charter, a copy of the charter, together with a statement setting forth the submission of the charter to the qualified electors and its ratification by them, shall be certified by the clerk of the board of supervisors and shall be submitted to the governor for approval. The governor shall approve the charter within thirty days after its submission if it is not in conflict with, or states that in the event of a conflict is subject to, this constitution and the laws of this state. On approval, the charter becomes the organic law of the county, and certified copies of the charter shall be filed in the office of the secretary of state and with the clerk of the board of supervisors after being recorded in the office of the county recorder. Thereafter all courts shall take judicial notice of the charter.

6. Amendment of charter

Section 6. A charter shall set forth procedures for amendment of the charter. Proposed amendments shall be submitted to the qualified electors of the county at a general or special election and become effective if ratified by a majority of the qualified electors voting on the amendments and approved by the governor in the manner provided for in section 5 of this article.

7. County charter provisions

Section 7. A. Charter counties continue to be political subdivisions of this state that exist to aid in the administration of this state's laws and for purposes of self-government. Except as otherwise provided in this article the powers of the legislature over counties are not affected by this section and sections 5, 6, 8 and 9 of this article. Charter counties shall provide the same state mandated services and perform the same state mandated functions as non-charter counties. Charter counties may exercise, if provided by the charter, all powers over local concerns of the county consistent with, and subject to, the constitution and the laws of this state. In matters of strictly local municipal concern, charters adopted pursuant to article XIII shall control in any case of conflict with a county charter adopted pursuant to this article.

B. If a county has framed and adopted a charter and the charter is approved by the governor as provided in this article, the county shall be governed by the terms of its charter and ordinances passed pursuant to its charter. If the charter has been framed, adopted and approved and any of its provisions are in conflict with any county ordinance, rule or regulation relating to local concerns of the counties in force at the time of the adoption and approval of the charter, the provisions of the charter prevail notwithstanding the conflict and operate as a repeal or suspension of the law to the extent of conflict, and the law is not thereafter operative as to such conflict.

C. Notwithstanding article IX, section 1, if proposed and approved in the charter, a charter county may levy and collect:

1. Taxes on a countywide basis to provide services on a countywide basis.

2. Taxes on a specially designated area basis to provide services or special levels of service to that area.

   All taxes levied pursuant to this subsection shall be uniform upon the same class of property within the territorial limits of the county or the specially designated area and shall be levied and collected for public purposes only.

D. The decision to include a charter provision authorizing taxation pursuant to subsection C, paragraph 1 or 2 of this section shall be placed on the ballot as separate questions at the election to ratify the charter and must be approved by a majority of the qualified electors voting at the election. The result of the voting on either provision authorizing taxation does not affect the result of the voting to ratify the charter. Charter provisions authorizing taxation pursuant to subsection C, paragraph 1 or 2 of this section may also be proposed by an amendment to the charter pursuant to section 6 of this article.

E. If the authority to tax pursuant to subsection C, paragraph 2 of this section is approved for inclusion in the charter, any new tax proposed by the county under subsection C, paragraph 2 of this section shall be voted on by the qualified electors of the specially designated area. The tax must be ratified by a majority vote of the qualified electors voting at the election.

F. A transaction privilege tax, use tax or similar tax levied by a county pursuant to subsection C, paragraph 1 of this section:

1. May be imposed on only those business activities, or on the use, storage or consumption, which are subject to the comparable state transaction privilege tax, use tax or similar tax.

2. Shall provide all exclusion and exemptions provided by, and administrative provisions consistent with, the comparable state transaction privilege tax, use tax or similar tax.

G. All taxes levied under subsection F of this section shall not exceed an aggregate rate of two per cent when combined with existing taxes levied pursuant to title 42, chapter 8.3.

H. If approved in the charter, a charter county may adopt fees and fee schedules for any county products and county service delivery it provides in the conduct of any official business. Notwithstanding any fee schedules or individual charges provided by state law, the governing body of a charter county may adopt an alternate fee schedule or individual charge. Any fee or charge established pursuant to this section shall be attributable to and defray or cover the current or future costs of the product or service delivery for which the fee or charge is assessed.

I. Taxes raised under the authority of this section shall be subject to the provisions of the county property tax and expenditure limitations pursuant to article IX, sections 19 and 20.

8. Government and other powers

Section 8. A. The county charter shall provide:

1. For an elective governing body and its method of compensation, its powers, duties and responsibilities, its authority to delegate powers, the method of election and removal of members, the terms of office and the manner of filling vacancies in the governing body.

2. For all officers established under section 3 of this article and article VI, section 23, and such additional officers as the charter may provide for, their election or appointment, consolidation or segregation, method of compensation, powers, duties and responsibilities, authority to delegate powers and, if elected, the method of election and removal, terms of office and the manner of filling vacancies in such offices. If the charter provides for the attorney to remain an elective officer of the county, the charter may provide for an appointive office to carry out the civil representation needs of the county, its departments, agencies, boards, commissions, officials and employees. If the elective governing body provided for in the charter does not consist of supervisors, the charter may provide for elimination of the office of supervisor. If the charter provides for the office of supervisor, the number of supervisors shall be not fewer than five or greater than nine. If the charter provides for the appointment or elimination of an officer established under section 3 of this article or article VI, section 23, or for an appointive office to carry out the civil representation needs of the county, those provisions shall include an effective date not earlier than the expiration of the term of office for the officer commencing in January immediately following the first general election at which the officer is elected following approval of the charter by the voters and shall be placed on the ballot as separate questions at the election to ratify the charter and must be approved by a majority of the qualified electors voting at the election. The result of the voting on any provisions authorizing appointment or elimination of officers does not affect the result of the voting to ratify the charter.

3. For the performance of functions required by statute.

4. For a periodic review of the charter provisions to be conducted at least once every ten years from the time of its ratification by the voters and the procedures for the periodic review.

B. The county charter may provide for other elective and appointive offices.

9. Self-executing provision

Section 9. The provisions of sections 5 through 8 of this article are self-executing, and no further legislation is required to make them effective.

Article XIII

MUNICIPAL CORPORATIONS

1. Incorporation and organization; classification

Section 1. Municipal corporations shall not be created by special laws, but the legislature, by general laws, shall provide for the incorporation and organization of cities and towns and for the classification of such cities and towns in proportion to population, subject to the provisions of this article.

2. Charter; preparation and proposal by board of freeholders; ratification and approval; amendment

Section 2. Any city containing, now or hereafter, a population of more than three thousand five hundred may frame a charter for its own government consistent with, and subject to, the Constitution and the laws of the state, in the following manner: A board of freeholders composed of fourteen qualified electors of said city may be elected at large by the qualified electors thereof, at a general or special election, whose duty it shall be, within ninety days after such election, to prepare and propose a charter for such city. Such proposed charter shall be signed in duplicate by the members of such board, or a majority of them, and filed, one copy of said proposed charter with the chief executive officer of such city and the other with the county recorder of the county in which said city shall be situated. Such proposed charter shall then be published in one or more newspapers published, and of general circulation, within said city for at least twenty-one days if in a daily paper, or in three consecutive issues if in a weekly paper, and the first publication shall be made within twenty days after the completion of the proposed charter. Within thirty days, and not earlier than twenty days, after such publication, said proposed charter shall be submitted to the vote of the qualified electors of said city at a general or special election. If a majority of such qualified electors voting thereon shall ratify such proposed charter, it shall thereupon be submitted to the governor for his approval, and the governor shall approve it if it shall not be in conflict with this Constitution or with the laws of the state. Upon such approval said charter shall become the organic law of such city and supersede any charter then existing (and all amendments thereto), and all ordinances inconsistent with said new charter. A copy of such charter, certified by the chief executive officer, and authenticated by the seal, of such city, together with a statement similarly certified and authenticated setting forth the submission of such charter to the electors and its ratification by them, shall, after the approval of such charter by the governor, be made in duplicate and filed, one copy in the office of the secretary of state and the other in the archives of the city after being recorded in the office of said county recorder. Thereafter all courts shall take judicial notice of said charter.

The charter so ratified may be amended by amendments proposed and submitted by the legislative authority of the city to the qualified electors thereof (or by petition as hereinafter provided), at a general or special election, and ratified by a majority of the qualified electors voting thereon and approved by the governor as herein provided for the approval of the charter.

3. Election of board of freeholders

Section 3. An election of such board of freeholders may be called at any time by the legislative authority of any such city. Such election shall be called by the chief executive officer of any such city within ten days after there shall have been filed with him a petition demanding such election, signed by a number of qualified electors residing within such city equal to twenty-five per centum of the total number of votes cast at the next preceding general municipal election. Such election shall be held not later than thirty days after the call therefor. At such election a vote shall be taken upon the question whether further proceedings toward adopting a charter shall be had in pursuance to the call, and unless a majority of the qualified electors voting thereon shall vote to proceed further, no further proceedings shall be had, and all proceedings up to the time of said election shall be of no effect.

4. Franchises; approval of electors; term

Section 4. No municipal corporation shall ever grant, extend, or renew a franchise without the approval of a majority of the qualified electors residing within its corporate limits who shall vote thereon at a general or special election, and the legislative body of any such corporation shall submit any such matter for approval or disapproval to such electors at any general municipal election, or call a special election for such purpose at any time upon thirty days' notice. No franchise shall be granted, extended, or renewed for a longer time than twenty-five years.

5. Right of municipal corporation to engage in business or enterprise

Section 5. Every municipal corporation within this state shall have the right to engage in any business or enterprise which may be engaged in by a person, firm, or corporation by virtue of a franchise from said municipal corporation.

6. Franchises; restrictions

Section 6. No grant, extension, or renewal of any franchise or other use of the streets, alleys, or other public grounds, or ways, of any municipality shall divest the state or any of its subdivisions of its or their control and regulation of such use and enjoyment; nor shall the power to regulate charges for public services be surrendered; and no exclusive franchise shall ever be granted.

7. Irrigation and other districts as political subdivisions

Section 7. Irrigation, power, electrical, agricultural improvement, drainage, and flood control districts, and tax levying public improvement districts, now or hereafter organized pursuant to law, shall be political subdivisions of the state, and vested with all the rights, privileges and benefits, and entitled to the immunities and exemptions granted municipalities and political subdivisions under this constitution or any law of the state or of the United States; but all such districts shall be exempt from the provisions of sections 7 and 8 of article IX of this constitution.

Article XIV

CORPORATION OTHER THAN MUNICIPAL

1. "Corporation" defined; right to sue and suability

Section 1. The term "corporation," as used in this article, shall be construed to include all associations and joint stock companies having any powers or privileges of corporations not possessed by individuals or co-partnerships, and all corporations shall have the right to sue and shall be subject to be sued, in all courts, in like cases as natural persons.

2. Formation under general laws; change of laws; regulation

Section 2. Corporations may be formed under general laws, but shall not be created by special acts. Laws relating to corporations may be altered, amended, or repealed at any time, and all corporations doing business in this state may, as to such business, be regulated, limited, and restrained by law.

3. Existing charters

Section 3. All existing charters under which a bona fide organization shall not have taken place and business commenced in good faith within six months from the time of the approval of this Constitution shall thereafter have no validity.

4. Restriction to business authorized by charter or law

Section 4. No corporation shall engage in any business other than that expressly authorized in its charter or by the law under which it may have been or may hereafter be organized.

5. Foreign corporations; transaction of business

Section 5. No corporation organized outside of the limits of this state shall be allowed to transact business within this state on more favorable conditions than are prescribed by law for similar corporations organized under the laws of this state; and no foreign corporation shall be permitted to transact business within this state unless said foreign corporation is by the laws of the country, state, or territory under which it is formed permitted to transact a like business in such country, state, or territory.

6. Stocks; bonds

Section 6. No corporation shall issue stock, except to bona fide subscribers therefor or their assignees; nor shall any corporation issue any bond, or other obligation, for the payment of money, except for money or property received or for labor done. The stock of corporations shall not be increased, except in pursuance of a general law, nor shall any law authorize the increase of stock of any corporation without the consent of the person or persons holding the larger amount in value of the stock of such corporation, nor without due notice of the proposed increase having been given as may be prescribed by law. All fictitious increase of stock or indebtedness shall be void.

7. Lease or alienation of franchise

Section 7. No corporation shall lease or alienate any franchise so as to relieve the franchise, or property held thereunder, from the liabilities of the lessor, or grantor, lessee, or grantee, contracted or incurred in the operation, use, or enjoyment of such franchise or of such franchise or of any of its privileges.

8. Filing of articles of incorporation; place of business; agent for service of process; venue

Section 8. No domestic or foreign corporation shall do any business in this state without having filed its articles of incorporation or a certified copy thereof with the corporation commission, and without having one or more known places of business and an authorized agent, or agents, in the state upon whom process may be served. Suit may be maintained against a foreign corporation in the county where an agent of such corporation may be found, or in the county where the cause of action may arise.

9. Eminent domain; taking corporate property and franchises for public use

Section 9. The right of exercising eminent domain shall never be so abridged or construed as to prevent the state from taking the property and the franchises of incorporated companies and subjecting them to public use the same as the property of individuals.

10. Elections for directors or managers

Section 10. In all elections for directors or managers of any corporation, each shareholder shall have the right to cast as many votes in the aggregate as he shall be entitled to vote in said company under its charter multiplied by the number of directors or managers to be elected at such election; and each shareholder may cast the whole number of votes, either in person or by proxy, for one candidate, or distribute such votes among two or more such candidates; and such directors or managers shall not be elected otherwise.

11. Liability of stockholders

Section 11. LIABILITY OF STOCKHOLDERS. The shareholders or stockholders of every banking or insurance corporation or association shall be held individually responsible, equally and ratably, and not one for another, for all contracts, debts, and engagements of such corporation or association, to the extent of the amount of their stock therein, at the par value thereof, in addition to the amount invested in such shares or stock; provided, however, that the shareholders or stockholders of any banking corporation or association which is a member of the federal deposit insurance corporation or any successor thereto or other insuring instrumentality of the United States in accordance with the provisions of any applicable law of the United States of America, shall not be liable for any amount in addition to the amount already invested in such shares or stock.

12. Officers of banking institutions; individual responsibility

Section 12. Any president, director, manager, cashier, or other officer of any banking institution who shall receive, or assent to, the reception of any deposits after he shall have knowledge of the fact that such banking institution is insolvent or in failing circumstances shall be individually responsible for such deposits.

13. Want of legal organization as a defense

Section 13. No persons acting as a corporation under the laws of Arizona shall be permitted to set up, or rely upon, the want of a legal organization as a defense to any action which may be brought against them as a corporation, nor shall any person or persons who may be sued on a contract now or hereafter made with such corporation, or sued for any injury now or hereafter done to its property, or for a wrong done to its interests, be permitted to rely upon such want of legal organization in his or their defense.

14. Legislative power to impose conditions

Section 14. This article shall not be construed to deny the right of the legislative power to impose other conditions upon corporations than those herein contained.

15. Monopolies and trusts

Section 15. Monopolies and trusts shall never be allowed in this state and no incorporated company, co-partnership or association of persons in this state shall directly or indirectly combine or make any contract, with any incorporated company, foreign or domestic, through their stockholders or the trustees or assigns of such stockholders or with any co-partnership or association of persons, or, in any manner whatever, to fix the prices, limit the production, or regulate the transportation of any product or commodity. The legislature shall enact laws for the enforcement of this section by adequate penalties, and in the case of incorporated companies, if necessary for that purpose, may, as a penalty declare a forfeiture of their franchises.

16. Records, books, and files; visitorial and inquisitorial powers of state

Section 16. The records, books, and files of all public service corporations, state banks, building and loan associations, trust, insurance, and guaranty companies shall be at all times liable and subject to the full visitorial and inquisitorial powers of the state, notwithstanding the immunities and privileges secured in the declaration of rights of this Constitution to persons, inhabitants, and citizens of this state.

17. Fees; reports; licensing of foreign corporations

Section 17. Provision shall be made by law for the payment of a fee to the state by every domestic corporation, upon the grant, amendment, or extension of its charter, and by every foreign corporation upon its obtaining a license to do business in this state; and also for the payment, by every domestic corporation and foreign corporation doing business in this state, of an annual registration fee of not less than ten dollars, which fee shall be paid irrespective of any specific license or other tax imposed by law upon such company for the privilege of carrying on its business in this state, or upon its franchise or property; and for the making, by every such corporation, at the time of paying such fee, of such report to the corporation commission of the status, business, or condition of such corporation, as may be prescribed by law. No foreign corporation, except insurers, shall have authority to do business in this state, until it shall have obtained from the corporation commission a license to do business in the state, upon such terms as may be prescribed by law. The legislature may relieve any purely charitable, social, fraternal, benevolent, or religious institution from the payment of such annual registration fee.

18. Contributions to influence elections or official action

Section 18. It shall be unlawful for any corporation, organized or doing business in this state, to make any contribution of money or anything of value for the purpose of influencing any election or official action.

19. Penalties for violation of article

Section 19. Suitable penalties shall be prescribed by law for the violation of any of the provisions of this article.

Article XV

THE CORPORATION COMMISSION

1. Term limits on corporation commission; composition; election; office vacancies; qualifications

Section 1. A. No member of the corporation commission shall hold that office for more than two consecutive terms. No corporation commissioner may serve again in that office until out of office for one full term. Any person who serves one half or more of a term shall be considered to have served one term for purposes of this section.

B. A corporation commission is hereby created to be composed of five persons who shall be elected at the general election, and whose term of office shall be four years, and who shall maintain their chief office at the state capital. The two additional commission members shall be elected at the 2002 general election for initial two-year terms beginning on the first Monday in January, 2003. Thereafter, all terms shall be four-year terms.

C. In case of vacancy in the office, the governor shall appoint a commissioner to fill the vacancy. The appointed commissioner shall fill the vacancy until a commissioner shall be elected at a general election as provided by law, and shall qualify. The qualifications of commissioners may be prescribed by law.

2. "Public service corporations" defined

Section 2. All corporations other than municipal engaged in furnishing gas, oil, or electricity for light, fuel, or power; or in furnishing water for irrigation, fire protection, or other public purposes; or in furnishing, for profit, hot or cold air or steam for heating or cooling purposes; or engaged in collecting, transporting, treating, purifying and disposing of sewage through a system, for profit; or in transmitting messages or furnishing public telegraph or telephone service, and all corporations other than municipal, operating as common carriers, shall be deemed public service corporations.

3. <u>Power of commission as to classifications, rates and charges, rules, contracts, and accounts; local regulation</u>

Section 3. The corporation commission shall have full power to, and shall, prescribe just and reasonable classifications to be used and just and reasonable rates and charges to be made and collected, by public service corporations within the state for service rendered therein, and make reasonable rules, regulations, and orders, by which such corporations shall be governed in the transaction of business within the state, and may prescribe the forms of contracts and the systems of keeping accounts to be used by such corporations in transacting such business, and make and enforce reasonable rules, regulations, and orders for the convenience, comfort, and safety, and the preservation of the health, of the employees and patrons of such corporations; Provided, that incorporated cities and towns may be authorized by law to exercise supervision over public service corporations doing business therein, including the regulation of rates and charges to be made and collected by such corporations; Provided further, that classifications, rates, charges, rules, regulations, orders, and forms or systems prescribed or made by said corporation commission may from time to time be amended or repealed by such commission.

4. <u>Power to inspect and investigate</u>

Section 4. The corporation commission, and the several members thereof, shall have power to inspect and investigate the property, books, papers, business, methods, and affairs of any corporation whose stock shall be offered for sale to the public and of any public service corporation doing business within the state, and for the purpose of the commission, and of the several members thereof, shall have the power of a court of general jurisdiction to enforce the attendance of witnesses and the production of evidence by subpoena, attachment, and punishment, which said power shall extend throughout the state. Said commission shall have power to take testimony under commission or deposition either within or without the state.

5. <u>Power to issue certificates of incorporation and licenses</u>

Section 5. The corporation commission shall have the sole power to issue certificates of incorporation to companies organizing under the laws of this state, and to issue licenses to foreign corporations to do business in this state, except as insurers, as may be prescribed by law.

Domestic and foreign insurers shall be subject to licensing, control and supervision by a department of insurance as prescribed by law. A director of the department of insurance shall be appointed by the governor with the consent of the senate in the manner prescribed by law for a term which may be prescribed by law.

6. Enlargement of powers by legislature; rules and regulations

Section 6. The law-making power may enlarge the powers and extend the duties of the corporation commission, and may prescribe rules and regulations to govern proceedings instituted by and before it; but, until such rules and regulations are provided by law, the commission may make rules and regulations to govern such proceedings.

7. Connecting and intersecting lines of transportation and communications corporations

Section 7. Every public service corporation organized or authorized under the laws of the state to do any transportation or transmission business within the state shall have the right to construct and operate lines connecting any points within the state, and to connect at the state boundaries with like lines; and every such corporation shall have the right with any of its lines to cross, intersect, or connect with, any lines of any other public service corporation.

8. Transportation by connecting carriers

Section 8. Every public service corporation doing a transportation business within the state shall receive and transport, without delay or discrimination, cars loaded or empty, property, or passengers delivered to it by any other public service corporation doing a similar business, and deliver cars, loaded or empty, without delay or discrimination, to other transportation corporations, under such regulations as shall be prescribed by the corporation commission, or by law.

9. Transmission of messages by connecting carriers

Section 9. Every public service corporation engaged in the business of transmitting messages for profit shall receive and transmit, without delay or discrimination, any messages delivered to it by any other public service corporation engaged in the business of transmitting messages for profit, and shall, with its lines, make physical connection with the lines of any public service corporation engaged in the business of transmitting messages for profit, under such rules and regulations as shall be prescribed by the corporation commission, or by law; Provided, that such public service corporations shall deliver messages to other such corporations, without delay or discrimination, under such rules and regulations as shall be prescribed by the corporation commission, or by law.

10. Railways as public highways; other corporations as common carriers

Section 10. Railways heretofore constructed, or that may hereafter be constructed, in this state, are hereby declared public highways and all railroads are declared to be common carriers and subject to control by law. All electric, transmission, telegraph, telephone, or pipeline corporations, for the transportation of electricity, messages, water, oil, or other property for profit, are declared to be common carriers and subject to control by law.

11. Movable property as personal property; liability of property to attachment, execution and sale

Section 11. The rolling stock and all other movable property belonging to any public service corporation in this state, shall be considered personal property, and its real and personal property, and every part thereof, shall be liable to attachment, execution, and sale in the same manner as the property of individuals; and the law-making power shall enact no laws exempting any such property from attachment, execution, or sale.

12. Charges for service; discrimination; free or reduced rate transportation

Section 12. All charges made for service rendered, or to be rendered, by public service corporations within this state shall be just and reasonable, and no discrimination in charges, service, or facilities shall be made between persons or places for rendering a like and contemporaneous service, except that the granting of free or reduced rate transportation may be authorized by law, or by the corporation commission, to the classes of persons described in the act of Congress approved February 11, 1887, entitled An Act to Regulate Commerce, and the amendments thereto, as those to whom free or reduced rate transportation may be granted.

13. Reports to commission

Section 13. All public service corporations and corporations whose stock shall be offered for sale to the public shall make such reports to the corporation commission, under oath, and provide such information concerning their acts and operations as may be required by law, or by the corporation commission.

14. Value of property of public service corporations

Section 14. The corporation commission shall, to aid it in the proper discharge of its duties, ascertain the fair value of the property within the state of every public service corporation doing business therein; and every public service corporation doing business within the state shall furnish to the commission all evidence in its possession, and all assistance in its power, requested by the commission in aid of the determination of the value of the property within the state of such public service corporation.

15. Acceptance of constitutional provisions by existing corporations

Section 15. No public service corporation in existence at the time of the admission of this state into the union shall have the benefit of any future legislation except on condition of complete acceptance of all provisions of this Constitution applicable to public service corporations.

16. Forfeitures for violations

Section 16. If any public service corporation shall violate any of the rules, regulations, orders, or decisions of the corporation commission, such corporation shall forfeit and pay to the state not less than one hundred dollars nor more than five thousand dollars for each such violation, to be recovered before any court of competent jurisdiction.

17. Appeal to courts

Section 17. Nothing herein shall be construed as denying to public service corporations the right of appeal to the courts of the state from the rules, regulations, orders, or decrees fixed by the corporation commission, but the rules, regulations, orders, or decrees so fixed shall remain in force pending the decision of the courts.

19. Power to impose fines

Section 19. The corporation commission shall have the power and authority to enforce its rules, regulations, and orders by the imposition of such fines as it may deem just, within the limitations prescribed in section 16 of this article.

Article XVI

MILITIA

1. Composition of militia

Section 1. The militia of the state of Arizona shall consist of all capable citizens of the state between the ages of eighteen and forty-five years, and of those between said ages who shall have declared their intention to become citizens of the United States, residing therein, subject to such exemptions as now exist, or as may hereafter be created, by the laws of the United States or of this state.

2. Composition and designation of organized militia

Section 2. The organized militia shall be designated "The National Guard of Arizona," and shall consist of such organized military bodies as now exist under the laws of the territory of Arizona or as may hereafter be authorized by law.

3. Conformity to federal regulations

Section 3. The organization, equipment, and discipline of the national guard shall conform as nearly as shall be practicable to the regulations for the government of the armies of the United States.

Article XVII

WATER RIGHTS

1. Riparian water rights

Section 1. The common law doctrine of riparian water rights shall not obtain or be of any force or effect in the state.

2. Recognition of existing rights

Section 2. All existing rights to the use of any of the waters in the state for all useful or beneficial purposes are hereby recognized and confirmed.

Article XVIII

LABOR

1. Eight-hour day

Section 1. Eight hours and no more, shall constitute a lawful day's work in all employment by, or on behalf of, the state or any political subdivision of the State. The legislature shall enact such laws as may be necessary to put this provision into effect, and shall prescribe proper penalties for any violations of said laws.

2. Child labor

Section 2. No child under the age of fourteen years shall be employed in any gainful occupation at any time during the hours in which the public schools of the district in which the child resides are in session; nor shall any child under sixteen years of age be employed underground in mines, or in any occupation injurious to health or morals or hazardous to life or limb; nor for more than eight hours in any day.

3. Contractual immunity of employer from liability for negligence

Section 3. It shall be unlawful for any person, company, association, or corporation to require of its servants or employees as a condition of their employment, or otherwise, any contract or agreement whereby such person, company, association, or corporation shall be released or discharged from liability or responsibility on account of personal injuries which may be received by such servants or employees while in the service or employment of such person, company, association, or corporation, by reason of the negligence of such person, company, association, corporation, or the agents or employees thereof; and any such contract or agreement if made, shall be null and void.

4. Fellow servant doctrine

Section 4. The common law doctrine of fellow servant, so far as it affects the liability of a master for injuries to his servant resulting from the acts or omissions of any other servant or servants of the common master is forever abrogated.

5. Contributory negligence and assumption of risk

Section 5. The defense of contributory negligence or of assumption of risk shall, in all cases whatsoever, be a question of fact and shall, at all times, be left to the jury.

6. Recovery of damages for injuries

Section 6. The right of action to recover damages for injuries shall never be abrogated, and the amount recovered shall not be subject to any statutory limitation.

7. Employer's liability law

Section 7. To protect the safety of employees in all hazardous occupations, in mining, smelting, manufacturing, railroad or street railway transportation, or any other industry the legislature shall enact an employer's liability law, by the terms of which any employer, whether individual, association, or corporation shall be liable for the death or injury, caused by any accident due to a condition or conditions of such occupation, of any employee in the service of such employer in such hazardous occupation, in all cases in which such death or injury of such employee shall not have been caused by the negligence of the employee killed or injured.

8. Workmen's compensation law

Section 8. The legislature shall enact a workmen's compensation law applicable to workmen engaged in manual or mechanical labor in all public employment whether of the state, or any political subdivision or municipality thereof as may be defined by law and in such private employments as the legislature may prescribe by which compensation shall be required to be paid to any such workman, in case of his injury and to his dependents, as defined by law, in case of his death, by his employer, if in the course of such employment personal injury to or death of any such workman from any accident arising out of and in the course of, such employment, is caused in whole, or in part, or is contributed to, by a necessary risk or danger of such employment, or a necessary risk or danger inherent in the nature thereof, or by failure of such employer, or any of his or its agents or employee or employees to exercise due care, or to comply with any law affecting such employment; provided that it shall be optional with any employee engaged in any such private employment to settle for such compensation, or to retain the right to sue said employer or any person employed by said employer, acting in the scope of his employment, as provided by this Constitution; and, provided further, in order to assure and make certain a just and humane compensation law in the state of Arizona, for the relief and protection of such workmen, their widows, children or dependents, as defined by law, from the burdensome, expensive and litigious remedies for injuries to or death of such workmen, now existing in the state of Arizona, and producing uncertain and unequal compensation therefor, such employee, engaged in such private employment, may exercise the option to settle for compensation by failing to reject the provisions of such workmen's compensation law prior to the injury, except that if the injury is the result of an act done by the employer or a person employed by the employer knowingly and purposely with the direct object of injuring another, and the act indicates a wilful disregard of the life, limb or bodily safety of employees, then such employee may, after the injury, exercise the option to accept compensation or to retain the right to sue the person who injured him.

The percentages and amounts of compensation provided in house bill no. 227 enacted by the seventh legislature of the state of Arizona, shall never be reduced nor any industry included within the provision of said house bill no. 227 eliminated except by initiated or referred measure as provided by this Constitution.

9. Blacklists

Section 9. The exchange, solicitation, or giving out of any labor "black list," is hereby prohibited, and suitable laws shall be enacted to put this provision into effect.

10. Employment of aliens

Section 10. No person not a citizen or ward of the United States shall be employed upon or in connection with any state, county or municipal works or employment; provided, that nothing herein shall be construed to prevent the working of prisoners by the state or by any county or municipality thereof on street or road work or other public work and that the provisions of this section shall not apply to the employment of any teacher, instructor, or professor authorized to teach in the United States under the teacher exchange program as provided by federal statutes enacted by the congress of the United States or the employment of university or college faculty members. The legislature shall enact laws for the enforcement and shall provide for the punishment of any violation of this section.

Article XIX

MINES

(Version amended by 1992 Proposition 101)

The office of mine inspector is hereby established. The legislature shall enact laws so regulating the operation and equipment of all mines in the state as to provide for the health and safety of workers therein and in connection therewith, and fixing the duties of said office. Upon approval of such laws by the governor, the governor, with the advice and consent of the senate, shall forthwith appoint a mine inspector, who shall serve until his successor shall have been elected at the first general election thereafter and shall qualify. Said successor and all subsequent incumbents of said office shall be elected at general elections, and shall serve for four years. The initial four year term shall be served by the mine inspector elected in the general election held in November, 1994.

Article XIX Ordinance

(Version amended by 1992 Proposition 107)

The office of mine inspector is hereby established. The legislature, at its first session, shall enact laws so regulating the operation and equipment of all mines in the state as to provide for the health and safety of workers therein and in connection therewith, and fixing the duties of said office. Upon approval of such laws by the governor, the governor, with the advice and consent of the senate, shall forthwith appoint a mine inspector, who shall serve until his successor shall have been elected at the first general election thereafter and shall qualify. Said successor and all subsequent incumbents of said office shall be elected at general elections, and shall serve for a term of two years. No mine inspector shall serve more than four consecutive terms in that office. No mine inspector, after serving the maximum number of terms, which shall include any part of a term served, may serve in the same office until out of office for no less than one full term. This limitation on the number of terms of consecutive service shall apply to terms of office beginning on or after January 1, 1993.

The following ordinance shall be irrevocable without the consent of the United States and the people of this state:

First. Toleration of religious sentiment

First. Perfect toleration of religious sentiment shall be secured to every inhabitant of this state, and no inhabitant of this state shall ever be molested in person or property on account of his or her mode of religious worship, or lack of the same.

Second. Polygamy

Second. Polygamous or plural marriages, or polygamous co-habitation, are forever prohibited within this state.

Third. Introduction of intoxicating liquors into Indian country

Third. The introduction of intoxicating liquors for resale purposes into Indian country is prohibited within this state until July 1, 1957.

Fourth. <u>Public lands; Indian lands</u>

Fourth. The people inhabiting this state do agree and declare that they forever disclaim all right and title to the unappropriated and ungranted public lands lying within the boundaries thereof and to all lands lying within said boundaries owned or held by any Indian or Indian tribes, the right or title to which shall have been acquired through or from the United States or any prior sovereignty, and that, until the title of such Indian or Indian tribes shall have been extinguished, the same shall be, and remain, subject to the disposition and under the absolute jurisdiction and control of the Congress of the United States.

Fifth. <u>Taxation</u>

Fifth. The lands and other property belonging to citizens of the United States residing without this state shall never be taxed at a higher rate than the lands and other property situated in this state belonging to residents thereof, and no taxes shall be imposed by this state on any lands or other property within an Indian reservation owned or held by any Indian; but nothing herein shall preclude the state from taxing as other lands and other property are taxed, any lands and other property outside of an Indian reservation owned or held by any Indian, save and except such lands as have been granted or acquired as aforesaid, or as may be granted or confirmed to any Indian or Indians under any act of Congress.

Sixth. <u>Territorial debts and liabilities</u>

Sixth. The debts and liabilities of the territory of Arizona, and the debts of the counties thereof, valid and subsisting at the time of the passage of the enabling act approved June 20, 1910, are hereby assumed and shall be paid by the state of Arizona, and the state of Arizona shall, as to all such debts and liabilities, be subrogated to all the rights, including rights of indemnity and reimbursement, existing in favor of said territory or of any of the several counties thereof, at the time of the passage of the said enabling act; Provided that nothing in this ordinance shall be construed as validating or in any manner legalizing any territory, county, municipal, or other bonds, obligations, or evidences of indebtedness of said territory or the counties or municipalities thereof which now are or may be invalid or illegal at the time the said state of Arizona is admitted as a state, and the legislature or the people of the state of Arizona shall never pass any law in any manner validating or legalizing the same.

Seventh. <u>Public school system; suffrage</u>

Seventh. Provisions shall be made by law for the establishment and maintenance of a system of public schools which shall be open to all the children of the state and be free from sectarian control, and said schools shall always be conducted in English.

The state shall never enact any law restricting or abridging the right of suffrage on account of race, color, or previous condition of servitude.

Eighth. <u>English language</u>

Eighth. The ability to read, write, speak, and understand the English language sufficiently well to conduct the duties of the office without the aid of an interpreter, shall be a necessary qualification for all state officers and members of the state legislature.

Ninth. <u>Location of state capital</u>

Ninth. The capital of the state of Arizona, until changed by the electors voting at an election provided for by the legislature for that purpose shall be at the city of Phoenix, but no such election shall be called or provided for prior to the thirty-first day of December, nineteen hundred and twenty-five.

Twelfth. <u>Lands granted to state</u>

Twelfth. The state of Arizona and its people hereby consent to all and singular the provisions of the enabling act approved June 20, 1910, concerning the lands thereby granted or confirmed to the state, the terms and conditions upon which said grants and confirmations are made, and the means and manner of enforcing such terms and conditions, all in every respect and particular as in the aforesaid enabling act provided.

Thirteenth. <u>Ordinance as part of constitution; amendment</u>

Thirteenth. This ordinance is hereby made a part of the Constitution of the state of Arizona, and no future constitutional amendment shall be made which in any manner changes or abrogates this ordinance in whole or in part without the consent of Congress.

Article XXI

MODE OF AMENDING

1. Introduction in legislature; initiative petition; election

Section 1. Any amendment or amendments to this constitution may be proposed in either house of the legislature, or by initiative petition signed by a number of qualified electors equal to fifteen per centum of the total number of votes for all candidates for governor at the last preceding general election. Any proposed amendment or amendments which shall be introduced in either house of the legislature, and which shall be approved by a majority of the members elected to each of the two houses, shall be entered on the journal of each house, together with the ayes and nays thereon. When any proposed amendment or amendments shall be thus passed by a majority of each house of the legislature and entered on the respective journals thereof, or when any elector or electors shall file with the secretary of state any proposed amendment or amendments together with a petition therefor signed by a number of electors equal to fifteen per centum of the total number of votes for all candidates for governor in the last preceding general election, the secretary of state shall submit such proposed amendment or amendments to the vote of the people at the next general election (except when the legislature shall call a special election for the purpose of having said proposed amendment or amendments voted upon, in which case the secretary of state shall submit such proposed amendment or amendments to the qualified electors at said special election,) and if a majority of the qualified electors voting thereon shall approve and ratify such proposed amendment or amendments in said regular or special election, such amendment or amendments shall become a part of this constitution. Until a method of publicity is otherwise provided by law, the secretary of state shall have such proposed amendment or amendments published for a period of at least ninety days previous to the date of said election in at least one newspaper in every county of the state in which a newspaper shall be published, in such manner as may be prescribed by law. If more than one proposed amendment shall be submitted at any election, such proposed amendments shall be submitted in such manner that the electors may vote for or against such proposed amendments separately.

2. Convention

Section 2. No Convention shall be called by the Legislature to propose alterations, revisions, or amendments to this Constitution, or to propose a new Constitution, unless laws providing for such Convention shall first be approved by the people on a Referendum vote at a regular or special election, and any amendments, alterations, revisions, or new Constitution proposed by such Convention shall be submitted to the electors of the State at a general or special election and be approved by the majority of the electors voting thereon before the same shall become effective.

Article XXII

SCHEDULE AND MISCELLANEOUS

1. Existing rights, actions, suits, proceedings, contracts, claims, or demands; process

Section 1. No rights, actions, suits, proceedings, contracts, claims, or demands, existing at the time of the admission of this State into the Union, shall be affected by a change in the form of government, from Territorial to State, but all shall continue as if no change had taken place; and all process which may have been issued under the authority of the Territory of Arizona, previous to its admission into the Union, shall be as valid as if issued in the name of the State.

2. Territorial laws

Section 2. All laws of the Territory of Arizona now in force, not repugnant to this Constitution, shall remain in force as laws of the State of Arizona until they expire by their own limitations or are altered or repealed by law; Provided, that wherever the word Territory, meaning the Territory of Arizona, appears in said laws, the word State shall be substituted.

3. Debts, fines, penalties, and forfeitures

Section 3. All debts, fines, penalties, and forfeitures which have accrued, or may hereafter accrue, to the Territory of Arizona shall inure to the State of Arizona.

4. Recognizances; bonds; estate; judgments; choses in action

Section 4. All recognizances heretofore taken, or which may be taken, before the change from a Territorial to a State government, shall remain valid, and shall pass to and may be prosecuted in the name of the State, and all bonds executed to the Territory of Arizona, or to any county or municipal corporation, or to any officer, or court, in his or its official capacity, shall pass to the State authorities and their successors in office for the uses therein expressed, and may be sued for and recovered accordingly; and all the estate, real, personal, and mixed, and all judgments, decrees, bonds, specialties, choses in action, and claims, demands or debts of whatever description, belonging to the Territory of Arizona, shall inure to and vest in the State of Arizona, and may be sued for and recovered by the State of Arizona in the same manner, and to the same extent, as the same might or could have been by the Territory of Arizona.

5. Criminal prosecutions and penal actions; offenses; penalties; actions and suits

Section 5. All criminal prosecutions and penal actions which may have arisen, or which may arise, before the change from a Territorial to a State government, and which shall then be pending, shall be prosecuted to judgment and execution in the name of the State. All offenses committed against the laws of the Territory of Arizona before the change from a Territorial to a State government, and which shall not be prosecuted before such change, may be prosecuted in the name, and by the authority, of the State of Arizona, with like effect as though such change had not taken place, and all penalties incurred and punishments inflicted shall remain the same as if this Constitution had not been adopted. All actions at law and suits in equity, which may be pending in any of the courts, of the Territory of Arizona at the time of the change from a Territorial to a State government, shall be continued and transferred to the court of the State, or of the United States, having jurisdiction thereof.

6. Territorial, district, county, and precinct officers

Section 6. All Territorial, district, county, and precinct officers who may be in office at the time of the admission of the State into the Union shall hold their respective offices until their successors shall have qualified, and the official bonds of all such officers shall continue in full force and effect while such officers remain in office.

7. Causes pending in district courts of territory; records, papers, and property

Section 7. Whenever the judge of the superior court of any county, elected or appointed under the provisions of this Constitution, shall have qualified, the several causes then pending in the district court of the Territory, and in and for such county, except such causes as would have been within the exclusive jurisdiction of the United States courts, had such courts existed at the time of the commencement of such causes within such county, and the records, papers, and proceedings of said district court, and other property pertaining thereto, shall pass into the jurisdiction and possession of the superior court of such county.

It shall be the duty of the clerk of the district court having custody of such papers, records, and property, to transmit to the clerk of said superior court the original papers in all cases pending in such district and belonging to the jurisdiction of said superior court, together with a transcript, or transcripts, of so much of the record of said district court as shall relate to the same; and until the district courts of the Territory shall be superseded in manner aforesaid, and as in this Constitution provided, the said district courts, and the judges thereof, shall continue with the same jurisdiction and powers, to be exercised in the same judicial district, respectively, as heretofore, and now, constituted.

8. Probate records and proceedings

Section 8. When the State is admitted into the Union, and the superior courts, in their respective counties, are organized, the books, records, papers, and proceedings of the probate court in each county, and all causes and matters of administration pending therein, shall pass into the jurisdiction and possession of the superior court of the same county created by this Constitution, and the said court shall proceed to final judgment or decree, order, or other determination, in the several matters and causes with like effect as the probate court might have done if this Constitution had not been adopted.

9. Causes pending in supreme court of territory; records, papers, and property

Section 9. Whenever a quorum of the judges of the Supreme Court of the State shall have been elected, and qualified, and shall have taken office, under this Constitution, the causes then pending in the Supreme Court of the Territory, except such causes as would have been within the exclusive jurisdiction of the United States courts, had such courts existed at the time of the commencement of such causes, and the papers, records, and proceedings of said court, and the seal and other property pertaining thereto, shall pass into the jurisdiction and possession of the Supreme Court of the State, and until so superseded, the Supreme Court of the Territory, and the judges thereof, shall continue, with like powers and jurisdiction as if this Constitution had not been adopted, or the State admitted into the Union; and all causes pending in the Supreme Court of the Territory at said time, and which said causes would have been within the exclusive jurisdiction of the United States courts, had such courts existed, at the time of the commencement of such causes, and the papers, records, and proceedings of said court, relating thereto, shall pass into the jurisdiction of the United States courts, all as in the Enabling Act approved June 20, 1910, provided.

10. Seals of supreme court, superior courts, municipalities, and county officers

Section 10. Until otherwise provided by law, the seal now in use in the Supreme Court of the Territory, shall be the seal of the Supreme Court of the State, except that the word "State", shall be substituted for the word "Territory" on said seal. The seal of the superior courts of the several counties of the State, until otherwise provided by law, shall be the vignette of Abraham Lincoln, with the words "Seal of the Superior Court The seal of municipalities, and of all county officers, in the Territory, shall be the seals of such municipalities and county officers, respectively, under the State, until otherwise provided by law, except that the word "Territory", or "Territory of Arizona", be changed to read "State" or "State of Arizona", where the same may appear on any such seals.

11. Effective date of constitution

Section 11. The provisions of this Constitution shall be in force from the day on which the President of the United States shall issue his proclamation declaring the State of Arizona admitted into the Union.

12. Election of representative in congress

Section 12. One Representative in the Congress of the United States shall be elected from the State at large, and at the same election at which officers shall be elected under the Enabling Act, approved June 20, 1910, and, thereafter, at such times and in such manner as may be prescribed by law.

13. Continuation in office until qualification of successor

Section 13. The term of office of every officer to be elected or appointed under this Constitution or the laws of Arizona shall extend until his successor shall be elected and shall qualify.

14. Initiative

Section 14. Any law which may be enacted by the Legislature under this Constitution may be enacted by the people under the Initiative. Any law which may not be enacted by the Legislature under this Constitution shall not be enacted by the people.

15. Public institutions

Section 15. Correctional and penal institutions, and institutions for the benefit of persons who have mental or physical disabilities and such other institutions as the public good may require, shall be established and supported by the State in such manner as may be prescribed by law.

16. Confinement of minor offenders

Section 16. It shall be unlawful to confine any minor under the age of eighteen years, accused or convicted of crime, in the same section of any jail or prison in which adult prisoners are confined. Suitable quarters shall be prepared for the confinement of such minors.

17. Compensation of public officers

Section 17. All State and county officers (except notaries public) and all justices of the peace and constables, whose precinct includes a city or town or part thereof, shall be paid fixed and definite salaries, and they shall receive no fees for their own use.

18. Nomination of incumbent public officers to other offices

Section 18. Except during the final year of the term being served, no incumbent of a salaried elective office, whether holding by election or appointment, may offer himself for nomination or election to any salaried local, State or federal office.

19. Lobbying

Section 19. The Legislature shall enact laws and adopt rules prohibiting the practice of lobbying on the floor of either House of the Legislature, and further regulating the practice of lobbying.

20. Design of state seal

Section 20. The seal of the State shall be of the following design: In the background shall be a range of mountains, with the sun rising behind the peaks thereof, and at the right side of the range of mountains there shall be a storage reservoir and a dam, below which in the middle distance are irrigated fields and orchards reaching into the foreground, at the right of which are cattle grazing. To the left in the middle distance on a mountain side is a quartz mill in front of which and in the foreground is a miner standing with pick and shovel. Above this device shall be the motto: "Ditat Deus." In a circular band surrounding the whole device shall be inscribed: "Great Seal of The State of Arizona", with the year of admission of the State into the Union.

21. Enactment of laws to carry constitution into effect

Section 21. The Legislature shall enact all necessary laws to carry into effect the provisions of this Constitution.

22. Judgments of death

Section 22. The judgment of death shall be inflicted by administering an intravenous injection of a substance or substances in a lethal quantity sufficient to cause death except that defendants sentenced to death for offenses committed prior to the effective date of the amendment to this section shall have the choice of either lethal injection or lethal gas. The lethal injection or lethal gas shall be administered under such procedures and supervision as prescribed by law. The execution shall take place within the limits of the state prison.

Article XXV

RIGHT TO WORK

Right to work or employment without membership in labor organization

No person shall be denied the opportunity to obtain or retain employment because of non-membership in a labor organization, nor shall the State or any subdivision thereof, or any corporation, individual or association of any kind enter into any agreement, written or oral, which excludes any person from employment or continuation of employment because of non-membership in a labor organization.

1. Powers of real estate broker or salesman

Section 1. Any person holding a valid license as a real estate broker or a real estate salesman regularly issued by the Arizona State Real Estate Department when acting in such capacity as broker or salesman for the parties, or agent for one of the parties to a sale, exchange, or trade, or the renting and leasing of property, shall have the right to draft or fill out and complete, without charge, any and all instruments incident thereto including, but not limited to, preliminary purchase agreements and earnest money receipts, deeds, mortgages, leases, assignments, releases, contracts for sale of realty, and bills of sale.

1. Regulation of ambulances; powers of legislature

Section 1. The legislature may provide for the regulation of ambulances and ambulance services in this state in all matters relating to services provided, routes served, response times and charges.

1. English as the official language; applicability

Section 1. (1) The English language is the official language of the state of Arizona.

(2) As the official language of this state, the English language is the language of the ballot, the public schools and all government functions and actions.

(3)(a) This article applies to:

(i) The legislative, executive and judicial branches of government.

(ii) All political subdivisions, departments, agencies, organizations, and instrumentalities of this state, including local governments and municipalities.

(iii) All statutes, ordinances, rules, orders, programs and policies.

(iv) All government officials and employees during the performance of government business.

(b) As used in this article, the phrase "this state and all political subdivisions of this state" shall include every entity, person, action or item described in this section, as appropriate to the circumstances.

2. <u>Requiring this state to preserve, protect and enhance English</u>

Section 2. This state and all political subdivisions of this state shall take all reasonable steps to preserve, protect and enhance the role of the English language as the official language of the state of Arizona.

3. <u>Prohibiting this state from using or requiring the use of languages other than English; exceptions</u>

Section 3. (1) Except as provided in subsection (2):

(a) This state and all political subdivisions of this state shall act in English and in no other language.

(b) No entity to which this article applies shall make or enforce a law, order, decree or policy which requires the use of a language other than English.

(c) No governmental document shall be valid, effective or enforceable unless it is in the English language.

(2) This state and all political subdivisions of this state may act in a language other than English under any of the following circumstances:

(a) To assist students who are not proficient in the English language, to the extent necessary to comply with federal law, by giving educational instruction in a language other than English to provide as rapid as possible a transition to English.

(b) To comply with other federal laws.

(c) To teach a student a foreign language as a part of a required or voluntary educational curriculum.

(d) To protect public health or safety.

(e) To protect the rights of criminal defendants or victims of crime.

4. Enforcement; standing

Section 4. A person who resides in or does business in this state shall have standing to bring suit to enforce this article in a court of record of the state. The legislature may enact reasonable limitations on the time and manner of bringing suit under this subsection.

1. Public retirement systems

Section 1. A. Public retirement systems shall be funded with contributions and investment earnings using actuarial methods and assumptions that are consistent with generally accepted actuarial standards.

B. The assets of public retirement systems, including investment earnings and contributions, are separate and independent trust funds and shall be invested, administered and distributed as determined by law solely in the interests of the members and beneficiaries of the public retirement systems.

C. Membership in a public retirement system is a contractual relationship that is subject to article II, section 25, and public retirement system benefits shall not be diminished or impaired.

Article XXVI

RIGHT OF LICENSED REAL ESTATE BROKERS AND SALESMEN TO PREPARE INSTRUMENTS INCIDENT TO PROPERTY TRANSACTIONS

1. Powers of real estate broker or salesman

Section 1. Any person holding a valid license as a real estate broker or a real estate salesman regularly issued by the Arizona State Real Estate Department when acting in such capacity as broker or salesman for the parties, or agent for one of the parties to a sale, exchange, or trade, or the renting and leasing of property, shall have the right to draft or fill out and complete, without charge, any and all instruments incident thereto including, but not limited to, preliminary purchase agreements and earnest money receipts, deeds, mortgages, leases, assignments, releases, contracts for sale of realty, and bills of sale.

Article XXVII

REGULATION OF PUBLIC HEALTH, SAFETY AND WELFARE

1. Regulation of ambulances; powers of legislature

Section 1. The legislature may provide for the regulation of ambulances and ambulance services in this state in all matters relating to services provided, routes served, response times and charges.

Article XXVIII

ENGLISH AS THE OFFICIAL LANGUAGE

1. English as the official language; applicability

Section 1. (1) The English language is the official language of the state of Arizona.

(2) As the official language of this state, the English language is the language of the ballot, the public schools and all government functions and actions.

(3)(a) This article applies to:

(i) The legislative, executive and judicial branches of government.

(ii) All political subdivisions, departments, agencies, organizations, and instrumentalities of this state, including local governments and municipalities.

(iii) All statutes, ordinances, rules, orders, programs and policies.

(iv) All government officials and employees during the performance of government business.

(b) As used in this article, the phrase "this state and all political subdivisions of this state" shall include every entity, person, action or item described in this section, as appropriate to the circumstances.

2. Requiring this state to preserve, protect and enhance English

Section 2. This state and all political subdivisions of this state shall take all reasonable steps to preserve, protect and enhance the role of the English language as the official language of the state of Arizona.

3. <u>Prohibiting this state from using or requiring the use of languages other than English; exceptions</u>

Section 3. (1) Except as provided in subsection (2):

(a) This state and all political subdivisions of this state shall act in English and in no other language.

(b) No entity to which this article applies shall make or enforce a law, order, decree or policy which requires the use of a language other than English.

(c) No governmental document shall be valid, effective or enforceable unless it is in the English language.

(2) This state and all political subdivisions of this state may act in a language other than English under any of the following circumstances:

(a) To assist students who are not proficient in the English language, to the extent necessary to comply with federal law, by giving educational instruction in a language other than English to provide as rapid as possible a transition to English.

(b) To comply with other federal laws.

(c) To teach a student a foreign language as a part of a required or voluntary educational curriculum.

(d) To protect public health or safety.

(e) To protect the rights of criminal defendants or victims of crime.

4. <u>Enforcement; standing</u>

Section 4. A person who resides in or does business in this state shall have standing to bring suit to enforce this article in a court of record of the state. The legislature may enact reasonable limitations on the time and manner of bringing suit under this subsection.

Article XXIX

PUBLIC RETIREMENT SYSTEMS

1. Public retirement systems

Section 1. A. Public retirement systems shall be funded with contributions and investment earnings using actuarial methods and assumptions that are consistent with generally accepted actuarial standards.

B. The assets of public retirement systems, including investment earnings and contributions, are separate and independent trust funds and shall be invested, administered and distributed as determined by law solely in the interests of the members and beneficiaries of the public retirement systems.

C. Membership in a public retirement system is a contractual relationship that is subject to article II, section 25, and public retirement system benefits shall not be diminished or impaired.

Sample Test

1. The boundaries of the state of Arizona can only be changed by:
    a. the legislature of Arizona and the adjoining states upon approval of the congress of the United States.
    b. a referendum on the ballot.
    c. the governors of the adjoining states.
    d. the governor of Arizona.

2. Arizona became a state in:
    a. 1860.
    b. 1912.
    c. 1929.
    d. 1875.

3. The power of government comes from the:
    a. military.
    b. law.
    c. people.
    d. governor.

4. Federal law takes precedence over:
    a. state law.
    b. county law.
    c. city law.
    d. all of the above.

5. People can express themselves freely
    a. in any way they want.
    b. in no way.
    c. as long as they don't abuse the right.
    d. all of the above.

6. Regarding religion and the state, it is true that:
    a. religion and the state must be separate.
    b. public moneys cannot be used for support of religion.
    c. there can be no religious requirements for office.
    d. all of the above.

7. The accused has the right to:
    a. a speedy trial.
    b. to call witnesses to testify on his behalf.
    c. to appeal if convicted.
    d. all of the above.

8. The branches of government are:
    a. public, courts and roads.
    (b.) executive, judicial and legislative.
    c. executive, senate and house.
    d. education, house and senate.

9. The Legislative branch is made up of:
    a. the courts and the senate.
    (b.) the senate and the house of representatives.
    c. the judicial and the house of representatives.
    d. None of the above.

10. The two methods of putting forth legislation through the voting process are:
    a. enactment and legislative.
    b. referendum and initiative.
    (c) referendum and enactment.
    d. initiative and enactment.

11. The governor cannot _____ a referendum or initiative measure passed by the people.
    a. vote for.
    (b.) veto.
    c. pass.
    d. Approve.

12. The House of Representatives has _____ from each district.
    a. one.
    (b.) Two.
    c. Three.
    d. Four.

13. The Senate has _____ members.
    a. Ten.
    (b.) twenty.
    c. thirty.
    d. Forty.

14. A special session of the legislature can be called by:
    (a.) presenting the governor with a petition signed by two-thirds of the members in each house.
    b. by scheduling the session with the appointments secretary.
    c. by arrangement among members of the house.
    d. By the secretary of state.

15. Redefining legislative districts is the function of the:
   a. House.
   b. Senate.
   c. independent redistricting commission.
   d. Secretary of state.

16. A member of the legislature must be a U.S. citizen and:
   a. twenty-one years old and an Arizona resident for one year
   b. twenty-five years old and an Arizona resident for two years.
   c. Twenty-five years old and an Arizona resident for three years.
   d. Thirty years old and an Arizona resident for four years.

17. Each annual session of the legislature begins:
   a. on the Monday following the Fourth of July.
   b. On the first Monday of January.
   c. On the second Monday of January.
   d. On the third Monday of January.

18. Each house establishes its own rules for its members and may expel them by:
   a. majority vote.
   b. Two-thirds vote.
   c. Three-fourths vote.
   d. One-half vote.

19. A bill must be:
   a. read three different times on three different days before it can be passed.
   b. Read once and voted upon.
   c. Voted on with or without a reading.
   d. Read on one day and voted on on another day.

20. There can be _____ subject per act
   a. one.
   b. Two.
   c. Three.
   d. Multiple.

21. Members of the legislature cannot serve more than _____ consecutive terms.
   a. one.
   b. Two.
   c. Three.
   d. Four.

22. Which office is not a member of the Executive branch?
    a. supreme court justice.
    b. Governor.
    c. Attorney general.
    d. State treasurer.

23. Officers of the Executive branch must be a U.S. citizen and at least:
    a. twenty-one years old and an Arizona resident for three years.
    b. Twenty-five years old and an Arizona resident for three years.
    c. Twenty-five years old and an Arizona resident for five years.
    d. Thirty years old and an Arizona resident for five years.

24. If the governor resigns or is removed from office who assumes the office until the
    holding of a special election.
    a. secretary of state.
    b. House majority leader.
    c. Attorney general
    d. Senate minority leader.

25. What is the minimum number of justices that are required on the Supreme Court?
    a. two.
    b. Three.
    c. Four.
    d. Five.

26. The normal term for a chief justice of the supreme court is:
    a. two years.
    b. Four years.
    c. Five years
    d. Six years.

27. The decisions of the supreme court are:
    a. privileged information.
    b. Available only to attorneys.
    c. Available only to judges.
    d. Available freely to the public.

28. Judges on the superior court are:
    a. elected by qualified voters.
    b. Appointed by the chief justice of the supreme court.
    c. Elected by members of the bar association.
    d. Appointed by the governor.

29. The courts of record are:
    a. any court is a court of record.
    b. The supreme court, the court of appeals and the superior court.
    c. The supreme court, the probate court and the court of justice.
    d. None of the above.

30. A judicial officer forfeits his office if he leaves the state for more than _____ without an extended leave of absence.
    a. fourteen days.
    b. Thirty days.
    c. Sixty days.
    d. None of the above.

31. Who can serve on more than one appointment committee?
    a. chief justice of the supreme court.
    b. Justice of the peace.
    c. Superior court judge.
    d. Court of appeals judge.

32. Voters must be:
    a. a United States citizen and twenty-one years of age.
    b. a United States citizen and eighteen years of age.
    c. A United States citizen and twenty years of age.
    d. None of the above.

33. In a primary election, an independent with now party affiliation:
    a. cannot vote.
    b. Can vote in either party's primary
    c. Can only vote an independent ballot.
    d. None of the above.

34. In criminal cases involving the death penalty:
    a. there is no jury allowed.
    b. The jury consists of six people.
    c. The jury must have twelve people.
    d. The jury must have ten people.

35. An elected officer can be removed from office by a process called:
    a. recall.
    b. Petition.
    c. Initiative.
    d. None of the above.

36. The house of representatives has the power of:
    a. firing members for non-attendance.
    b. Impeachment.
    c. Dismissal.
    d. Recall.

37. Taxes on a specific class of property:
    a. cannot be assigned.
    b. Must be arbitrarily assigned.
    c. Must be uniformly assigned.
    d. Are not collectible.

38. Property subject to taxation includes:
    a. all of federal, state, county and municipal property.
    b. None of federal, state, county and municipal property.
    c. All of federal, county and municipal property.
    d. Only federal property.

39. Widowers and the disabled can:
    a. be exempt from property tax depending of the assessment limit and their income.
    b. must pay all taxes no matter what the assessment limit is if they have any income.
    c. are exempt from property tax regardless of income and assessment.
    d. None of the above

40. Incorporated towns:
    a. can levy special assessments to make local improvements.
    b. Cannot levy special assessments unless it is for schools.
    c. Can only petition the legislature to raise taxes.
    d. Can only impose taxes that the voters vote on.

41. The debts of the unified school district cannot exceed more than _____ of the taxable property.
    a. ten.
    b. Twenty.
    c. Thirty.
    d. Forty.

42. Car owners face:
    a. an ad valorem tax property tax.
    b. A license tax.
    c. A tax based on the age of the driver.
    d. No tax.

43. The economic estimates commission:
    a. estimates state revenues.
    b. Estimates total personal income for the coming year.
    c. Estimates tax revenues.
    d. Estimates federal revenues.

44. The property valuation protection option is available:
    a. to families with children.
    b. To first-time home-owners.
    c. Only on second homes.
    d. Only to those sixty-five and older who qualify.

45. The ad valorem tax yearly increase can't exceed:
    a. one percent.
    b. Two percent.
    c. Five percent.
    d. Ten percent.

46. An increase in state taxes requires:
    a. a referendum by the voters.
    b. A simple majority vote in the legislature.
    c. A two-thirds vote of each house in the legislature.
    d. A three-fourths vote of each house in the legislature.

47. The state can lease agricultural lands for a period of:
    a. one year.
    b. Five years.
    c. Ten years.
    d. Twenty years.

48. The state can lease lands for mineral purposes for a period of:
    a. one year.
    b. Five years.
    c. Ten years.
    d. Twenty years.

49. The Constitution requires that the state provide for:
    a. kindergarten, common schools, high schools, normal schools, industrial schools, and universities, in addition to schools for the hearing and vision impaired.
    b. Only kindergarten, common schools and high schools.
    c. Only kindergarten, common schools, high schools, normal schools, industrial schools.
    d. Only kindergarten, common schools, high schools, normal schools, industrial schools, and universities.

50. The school system is run by:
    a. the county board of supervisors.
    b. Only a state board of education.
    c. Only a state board of education and a state superintendent of public instruction.
    d. a state board of education, a state superintendent of public instruction, county school superintendents, and governing boards for the state institutions.

51. The university is governed by:
    a. board of regents.
    b. County board of supervisors.
    c. The legislature.
    d. None of the above.

52. The county school fund is provided for by:
    a. laws of the legislature.
    b. The state highway tax.
    c. The license tax.
    d. Ad valorem tax.

53. Counties are:
    a. independent entities.
    b. Counties of the state.
    c. Counties of the municipality.
    d. None of the above.

54. County officers are:
    a. sheriff, a county attorney, a recorder, a treasurer, an assessor, a superintendent of schools and at least three supervisors.
    b. sheriff, county attorney and a recorder only.
    c. Sheriff, county attorney and an assessor only.
    d. Sheriff, county attorney, recorder and assessor only.

55. County officers are:
    a. appointed by the governor.
    b. Appointed by the legislature.
    c. Elected by the voters.
    d. Appointed by the county supervisor.

56. A county charter:
    a. determines the county name.
    b. becomes the organic law of the county.
    c. Determines the county personnel.
    d. Comes from the legislature.

57. Impeachment trials are held in the:
    a. supreme court.
    b. House of representatives.
    c. Senate.
    d. Superior court.

58. Municipal corporations can be formed:
    a. by anyone.
    b. By the city.
    c. By the county.
    d. By the legislature.

59. The county charter:
    a. Must be ratified by the voters of the county.
    b. Must be ratified by the voters of the state.
    c. Does not require ratification by any voters.
    d. None of the above.

60. Municipal corporations:
    a. Cannot be exclusive franchises.
    b. Can be exclusive franchises.
    c. Can be common franchises.
    d. Cannot exist.

61. Corporations:
    a. Require a charter.
    b. Can be sued.
    c. Cannot engage in business not stated in their charter.
    d. All of the above.

62. A president, director, manager, cashier or other officer of a bank:
    a. Can never be held personally responsible for accepting deposits.
    b. Can be held personally responsible for accepting deposits if they know the bank is failing.
    c. Only the president of the bank can be held personally responsible for accepting deposits if they know the bank is failing.
    d. None of the above.

63. Arizona law:
    a. Allows monopolies only.
    b. Allows trusts only.
    c. Allows monopolies and trusts.
    d. Allows neither monopolies nor trusts.

64. Corporations can:
    a. Not operate without paying an annual fee.
    b. Must pay an annual fee.
    c. Are not covered by law.
    d. None of the above.

65. Corporations:
    a. Can financially support the political candidate of their choice directly.
    b. Cannot make contributions to political campaigns.
    c. Can run paid advertisements for candidates of their choice.
    d. None of the above.

66. The Corporation Commission:
    a. Regulates the different forms of business in Arizona.
    b. Regulates all of the corporations in Arizona.
    c. Regulates public service corporations in Arizona.
    d. All of the above.

67. A public service corporation:
    a. Is a municipal corporation.
    b. Are corporations that are not municipal and that furnish gas, oil, electricity, sewers, telephone and common carriers.
    c. Are public corporations.
    d. Are owned by municipalities.

68. The Corporation Commission:
    a. Determines the rates charged by the public service corporations.
    b. Runs the public service corporations.
    c. Owns the public service corporations.
    d. None of the above.

69. The militia:
    a. Consists of all capable citizens between the ages of eighteen and forty-five years.
    b. Is known as "The National Guard of Arizona".
    c. Must conform to the regulations of the United States military.
    d. All of the above.

70. Water rights in Arizona:
    a. Don't exist.
    b. Are controlled by the common law of riparian water rights.
    c. Are not controlled by the common law of riparian water rights.
    d. None of the above.

71. Labor law in Arizona:
    a. Does not regulate the number of hours in the work day.
    b. Requires an eight hour work day.
    c. Requires a ten hour work day.
    d. None of the above.

72. A child fourteen or under:
    a. Cannot work for money during the hours of the school day.
    b. Can work part-time at any time of the day.
    c. Cannot work.
    d. Can work an eight hour workday.

73. The defense of contributory negligence is determined:
    a. By the employer.
    b. By the employee.
    c. By the jury.
    d. Is indeterminate.

74. A worker injured while in the service of an employer:
    a. Has the right to recover damages for injuries and the amount is not subject to any statutory limitation.
    b. Has no right to recover damages.
    c. Has a right to recover partial damages.
    d. Works at his own risk.

75. Under the employer's liability law and employer:
    a. Is automatically cleared of any responsibility for an employee's injury or death.
    b. Is liable for the death or injury of an employee incurred while working in the service of the employer where there is no negligence on the part of the employee.
    c. Faces criminal charges.
    d. None of the above.

76. Worker blacklists:
    a. Are illegal.
    b. Are legal.
    c. Are legal only if the worker quit.
    d. None of the above.

77. The purpose of the workmen's compensation law is:
   a. To provide pensions to retired workers.
   b. To provide compensation to the workman or his dependents if he is injured or killed while working.
   c. To provide jobs for unemployed workers.
   d. None of the above.

78. Arizona law:
   a. Sanctions polygamy.
   b. Outlaws polygamy.
   c. Requires polygamists to register with the county.
   d. None of the above.

79. Out-of-State people who own land in Arizona:
   a. Pay no taxes on their land.
   b. Pay higher taxes on their land.
   c. Cannot be charged higher taxes on their land.
   d. Pay special taxes on their land.

80. Property on Indian reservations:
   a. Is not taxed by the state.
   b. Is taxed at the same rate by the state.
   c. Is taxed at a higher rate by the state.
   d. Is taxed at a lower rate by the state.

81. The capital of Arizona is:
   a. Flagstaff.
   b. Tucson.
   c. Phoenix.
   d. Mesa.

82. In Arizona, public school education is:
   a. Open to all children of the state.
   b. Free of sectarian control.
   c. Conducted in English.
   d. All of the above.

83. Incumbents of a salaried elective office:
   a. Can run for any office at any time.
   b. Cannot run for election to any salaried local, state or federal office without first resigning their position unless it is the final year of their term.
   c. Cannot resign their current post to run for another.
   d. None of the above.

84. Lobbyists:
    a. Can engage in their lobbyist's duties anywhere they want.
    b. Can lobby on the floor of the house and senate.
    c. Can lobby on the floor of the house but not on the floor of the senate.
    d. Can't lobby on the floors of the house or the senate.

85. A person cannot be denied the right to work because he/she:
    a. Doesn't belong to a labor union.
    b. Isn't qualified for the job.
    c. Doesn't speak English.
    d. None of the above.

86. A person with a valid real estate broker's or salesman's license:
    a. Needs an attorney to complete the purchase agreement.
    b. Is qualified to complete the purchase agreement.
    c. Can complete transactions with a purchase agreement.
    d. None of the above.

87. Public retirement funds must be:
    a. Guaranteed by the legislature.
    b. Must be separate and independent.
    c. Must be approved by the legislature.
    d. Must be managed by the legislature.

88. A victim of a crime has the right:
    a. To be present at any proceedings.
    b. To be treated with dignity, respect and fairness.
    c. To be advised if the accused or convicted person is released.
    d. All of the above.

88. Laws can:
    a. Be written for any reason.
    b. Can be written granting privileges or immunity for one person.
    c. Cannot be written granting privileges or immunity for one person.
    d. None of the above.

89. Laws:
    a. Must apply equally to all people and corporations.
    b. Can give special treatment to Arizona residents.
    c. Can give special treatment to Arizona corporations.
    d. None of the above.

90. Property can be taken for public use:
    a. Without compensation.
    b. With below market compensation.
    c. With just compensation.
    d. By executive decree.

91. A bill of attainder is when:
    a. The county sends out tax bills.
    b. A law is enacted retroactively to declare a person guilty of a crime.
    c. Any law is enacted.
    d. A bill is vetoed.

92. Laws:
    a. Cannot be enacted granting privileges, compensation or powers based on hereditary.
    b. Can be enacted granting privileges, compensation or powers based on hereditary.
    c. Can be enacted granting special privileges.
    d. None of the above.

93. An indictment for a felony:
    a. Can take place at any time.
    b. Can take place upon arrest.
    c. Cannot happen without a preliminary hearing before a magistrate.
    d. Cannot happen without a supreme court ruling.

94. Initiative and referendum measures become law:
    a. By a majority vote in the legislature.
    b. By a two-thirds vote in each house in the legislature.
    c. By a three-fourths vote in each house in the legislature.
    d. By a majority vote in an election with the approval of the governor.

95. The power of initiative and referendum are available to:
    a. The people if they petition with the required number of signatures.
    b. Incorporated cities and towns and counties.
    c. Both of the above.
    d. None of the above.

96. An independent redistricting commission can be established:
    a. At any time the governor call for such a commission.
    b. At any time the legislature calls for such a commission.
    c. At any time a county calls for such a commission.
    d. In any year ending in a one.

97. A member of the legislature:
  a. Must be a city employee.
  b. Must be a county employee.
  c. Must be a federal employee.
  d. Cannot hold any other position with the state of Arizona or city or county except for school trustee or teacher.

98. A member of the legislature:
  a. Cannot be held civilly or criminally liable for anything said in the legislature.
  b. Can be held civilly or criminally liable for anything said in the legislature.
  c. Can be held civilly liable but not criminally liable for anything said in the legislature.
  d. Can be held criminally liable but not civilly liable for anything said in the legislature.

99. A quorum:
  a. Is only needed on special occasions.
  b. Is required for each house to do business.
  c. Can be done away with.
  d. None of the above.

100. In an election for Executive branch officers, if there is a tie:
  a. The chief justice of the supreme court decides the winner.
  b. There must be a second election.
  c. The two houses of the legislature elect one of the people.
  d. None of the above.

Answer Key

1. A   Article I, Section 2
2. B
3. C   Article II, Section 2
4. D   Article II, Section 3
5. C   Article II, Section 6
6. D   Article II, Section 12
7. D   Article II, Section 24
8. B   Article III
9. B   Article III, Section 1
10. C   Article III, Sections 2 and 3
11. B   Article III, Section 6a
12. B   Article III, Section 2, I
13. B   Article III, Section 2, 1
14. A   Article III, Section 2, 1, 2
15. C   Article III, Section 1, 3
16. C   Article III, Section 2
17. C   Article III, Section 3
18. B   Article III, Section 11
19. A   Article III, Section 12
20. A   Article III, Section 13
21. D   Article III, Section 21
22. A   Article V, Section 1a
23. C   Article V, Section 2
24. A   Article V, Section 6
25. D   Article VI, Section 2
26. D   Article VI, Section 4
27. D   Article VI, Section 8
28. A   Article VI, Section 12
29. B   Article VI, Section 30
30. C   Article VI, Section 34
31. A   Article VI, Section 36 b
32. B   Article VII, Section 2a
33. B   Article VII, Section 10
34. C   Article XXII, Section 22
35. A   Article VIII, Section 1
36. B   Article VIII, Section 6, 2, 1
37. C   Article IX, Section 1
38. B   Article IX, Section 2, 1
39. A   Article IX, Section 2.1, 2.2
40. A   Article IX, Section 6
41. C   Article IX, Section 8.1
42. B   Article IX, Section 11

43. B   Article IX, Section 17 (1)
44. D   Article IX, Section 18, 7
45. B   Article IX, Section 19, (1)
46. C   Article IX, Section 22
47. C   Article X, Section 3, 1
48. D   Article X, Section 3. 2
49. A   Article XI, Section 1
50. D   Article XI, Section 2
51. A   Article XI, Section 5
52. A   Article XI, Section 9
53. B   Article XII, Section 2
54. A   Article XII, Section 3
55. C   Article XII, Section 3
56. B   Article XII, Section 5
57. C   Article IX, Section 2.2
58. D   Article XIII, Section 1
59. A   Article XIII, Section 2
60. A   Article XIII, Section 6
61. D   Article XIV, Section 1
62. B   Article XIV, Section 12
63. D   Article XIV, Section 15
64. A   Article XIV, Section 17
65. B   Article XIV, Section 18
66. C   Article XV, Section 3
67. B   Article XV, Section 2
68. A   Article, XV, Section 3
69. D   Article XVI, Sections 1, 2, 3
70. C   Article XVII, Section 1
71. B   Article XVIII, Section 1
72. A   Article XVIII, Section 2
73. C   Article XVIII, Section 5
74. A   Article XVIII, Section 6
75. B   Article XVIII, Section 7
76. A   Article XVIII, Section 9
77. B   Article XVIII, Section 8
78. B   Article XIX, Second
79. C   Article XIX, Fifth
80. A   Article XIX, Fifth
81. C   Article XIX, Ninth
82. D   Article XIX, Seventh
83. B   Article XXII, Section 18
84. D   Article XXII, Section 19
85. A   Article XXV
86. B   Article XXV, Section 1
87. B   Article XXV, Section4, 1
88. D   Article II, Section 2.1

89. A Article II, Section 13
90. C Article II, Section 17
91. B Article II, Section 25
92. A Article II, Section 29
93. C Article II, Section 30
94. D Article IV, Section 1, 3
95. C Article IV, Section 1, 8
96. D Article IV, Section 1, 2, 3
97. D Article IV, Section 2, 2
98. A Article IV, Section 2, 6
99. B Article IV, Section 2, 9
100.C Article V, Section 1B

County Map of Arizona

Legislative District Map of Arizona

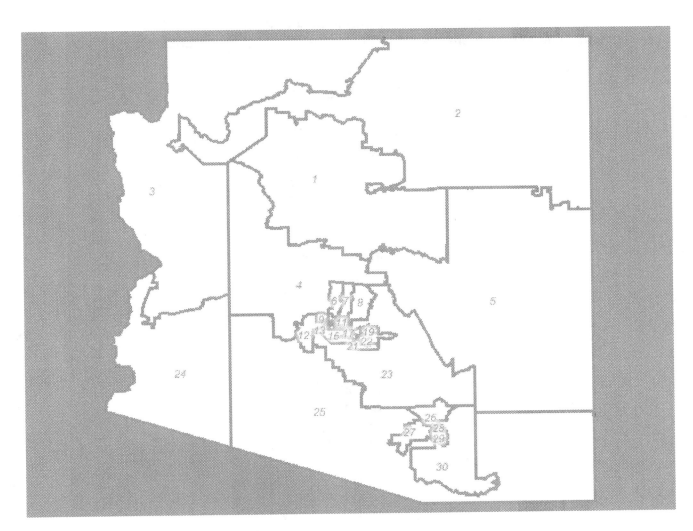

Map produced online from www.azredistricting.org

Study Aids

The Three Branches of Government

There are three branches of government, according to Article III Distribution of power. Listed below are the offices or bodies that belong to each branch.

Executive Branch

Governor
Secretary of State
Attorney General
State Treasurer
Superintendent of Public Instruction

Legislative

House of Representatives
Senate

Judicial

Supreme Court
Court of Appeals
Superior Court
Courts Not of Record